LAND ENTRIES
of
TRYON COUNTY
and
LINCOLN COUNTY
NORTH CAROLINA

- 1778-1780 -

Compiled by:
Dr. A.B. Pruitt

Southern Historical Press, Inc.
Greenville, South Carolina

This volume was reproduced
from a personal copy located in
the Publishers private library

Please direct all correspondence and book orders to:
www.southernhistoricalpress.com
or
SOUTHERN HISTORICAL PRESS, Inc.
1071 Park West Blvd.
Greenville, SC   29611

Southernhistoricalpress@gmail.com

Originally Copyright: Albert Bruce Pruitt, 1987
Copyright Transferred 2026 to:
    Southern Historical Press, Inc.
ISBN #978-0-94499-200-5
Printed in the United Sattes of America

INTRODUCTION

This book contains abstracts of 763 land entries in Tryon (later Lincoln) County, North Carolina from 1778 to 1780. The original book is in the North Carolina Archives in Rutherford County records (call number CR 086.404.1) because Rutherford County supplied the book to the Archives. The entries indicated the land as "in Tryon County" from Jan. 26, 1778 (entry #1) until May 1779 (entry #666) whereupon the land is "in Lincoln County" (entries 667-763). The book has been rebound and the pages laminated by the Archives.

Tryon County was formed in 1769 from Mecklenburg County. Mecklenburg County was formed in 1762 from Anson County. In 1779 Tryon County was abolished and Lincoln and Rutherford Counties took its place. Tryon County encompassed present day Burke, Cleveland, Gaston, Henderson, Lincoln, McDowell, & Rutherford Counties in North Carolina and several South Carolina counties. The entries in this book begin after the 1772 survey to determine the North Carolina-South Carolina boundary. So it is assumed that none of the land is in South Carolina. But several entries do indicate they are on the South Carolina border or "line of the South state". Old Lincoln County encompassed all or parts of the present counties of Catawba, Cleveland, Gaston, & Lincoln. Thus earlier records for people living in Old Lincoln Co may be found in Tryon, Mecklenburg, Rowan, or Anson Counties back to the 1750s.

An entry is a claim made to the appointed entry taker by the enterer for vacant or unclaimed land which was technically the property of the State. The enterer described the land--number of acres, nearby waterways, & neighboring land holders. If there were no problems, the entry taker issued a warrant to the county surveyor to survey the land. The warrant and survey may also describe the land and give additional land marks not mentioned in the original entry. The warrant and completed survey were sent to the Secretary of State. A grant or patent was then issued, and the person receiving the grant usually had about twelve months to register the grant in the county.

However, problems or counter claims did often appear. Some of these problems were:
(1) A "caveat" could be issued (after the entry and before the grant) to stop the grant from being issued. The person making a caveat could say he already owned part or all of the land. The entry taker usually indicated in the entry book if a caveat was made against all or part of an entry an entry and who made the caveat. Then a jury would settle the dispute. This decision could be: (a) in favor of the caveator in which case the entry was void or discontinued or the enterer withdrew the entry and the caveater did nothing more; or (b) in favor of the caveator for part of

the entry and the caveator retained his part of the land and the enterer obtained a grant for the remainder; or (c) in favor of the caveator and the caveator made a later entry on the land and obtained a grant; or (d) in favor of the enterer so he gets a grant for the land.

(2) After the entry was made and the warrant issued, the surveyor may encounter problems finding enough vacant land. This problems was usually resolved by changing the entry so the number of acres matched the survey. The entry taker often made corrections in the entry book in the case of shortages by writing the new number on top of the original entry.

(3) Fees were required to cover the entry, warrant, survey, & grant. If any fee was not paid, the entry was usually discontinued or abandoned and the land was still "vacant" for someone to claim. This later claim may be (a) by a later numbered entry or (b) by using the same entry number and the entry taker wrote the new name on top of the original name.

(4) In addition to the above problems, the entry taker may have made normal mistakes while writing in the entry book. So some "write overs" indicated in my abstracts may be due to entry taker's error and some may be due to problems encountered during the process of obtaining the grant.

In my abstracts, I have tried to adhere to the following format:

(a) Entry number; sometimes two entries had the same number (see #95 for example); the second entry was designated "[95A]" for the index.

(b) Whether "granted", "discontinued", "caveated", etc which the entry taker wrote in the left margin beside the entry number; "(blank)" indicates nothing was indicated by the entry taker.

(c) Name of person making the entry or claim; number of acres; and description of the land (usually) in this order: waterways, neighboring land owners (following the word "border"), roads, etc, and an indication if any "improvement" was mentioned.

(d) "entered" followed by the date.

(e) The amount of fees collected--sometimes omitted in later entries.

The punctuation is almost entirely mine and is included to aid the reader and divide the parts of the entry as indicated above.

If you find an "interesting" land entry, please write the Land Office (part of the Secretary of State's Office) NOT the North Carolina Archives.

Give the person's name and county because that's how things are filed there. If the grant was completed, there will probably (but not always) be a copy of the warrant for survey and the survey in the Land Office. These latter two documents may be more helpful than the land entry in locating the land. Using the entry, warrant, & survey, it is much easier to find the land and determine you have the correct grant when the number of acres change after the original entry.

If you know a person owned land in Tryon County, do not despair if you don't find an entry for him in this book. Many entries were made when the land was a part of Mecklenburg or Anson Counties. Very few of the entries prior to 1778 survive in an of these three counties. But the warrant and/or survey may exist in the Land Office (part of the Secretary of State's Office--not the Archives). Or the grant may survive in the Land Office or county deeds. So, the entry may be lost, but the grant might still exist. When writing the Land Office, send the person's name and county or counties where he lived because that's how things are filed.

This book does contain all the land entries found in the North Carolina Archives for Tryon County. There are many later entries for the present counties which were a part of Tryon County, some as recent as the early 1900s. Abstracts of the entries for Old Lincoln County may appear in a subsequent book as time and money permit.

A typed index on loose sheets is paper clipped to the front of the original book. This index includes almost every name and road in the entries, not just an index of enterers. The handwriting in the original book leaves something to be desired. So please allow extra latitude in the spelling of names due to the difficulty in interpretating handwriting. When in doubt, I have consulted the typed index and attempted to use the same spelling as is in the typed index.

An explanation concerning entries (usually for 1,000 to 3,000 ac) that refer to iron works: An act was passed by the North Carolina Assembly on Feb. 3, 1788 in Fayetteville. The act can be found in North Carolina Colonial & State Records (by Wm L. Saunders and Walter Clark) vol 24 p. 978. The act is mentioned as it passed through the Assembly in North Carolina Colonial Records vol. 20 p. 166, 533, 559, and 576. By this act a person was allowed to claim 3,000 ac of vacant land "not fit for cultivation". A jury of twelve people was then suppose to "view" the land to make sure it wasn't fit for cultivation. The person making the entry then had to "make it appear to the court" than he had produced 5,000 "wt" of iron in three years. When the court agreed, the county's entry taker issued a warrant, a survey was made, and a grant was issued. If the iron isn't produced, the land was to revert to the state. There is no mention of less than 3,000 ac, but presumably a 1,000 ac claim or grant would require less iron to be produced.

Please refer to North Carolina Research Genealogy and Local History by H. F. M. Leary and M. R. Stirewalt for additional information about land entries and the land granting process in North Carolina. Also this book contains a dictionary of legal terms often encountered in genealogical work as well as almost everything a genealogist needs to know about North Carolina research.

The author wishes to thank the North Carolina Archives for preserving this book and thank the staff for their courteous retrieval of the book from the stacks. He would also like to thank the people who brought forth affordable computers, printers, and software without which the preparation of this book would have been much more arduous.

The map with accompanies this book is included to help the reader locate the creeks which are mentioned most often in the index. The creek locations are not meant to be exact. More complete and accurate maps of the countries can be obtained from the North Carolina Department of Transportation or in a book of maps for all North Carolina counties from County Maps, Puetz place, Lyndon Station, WI.

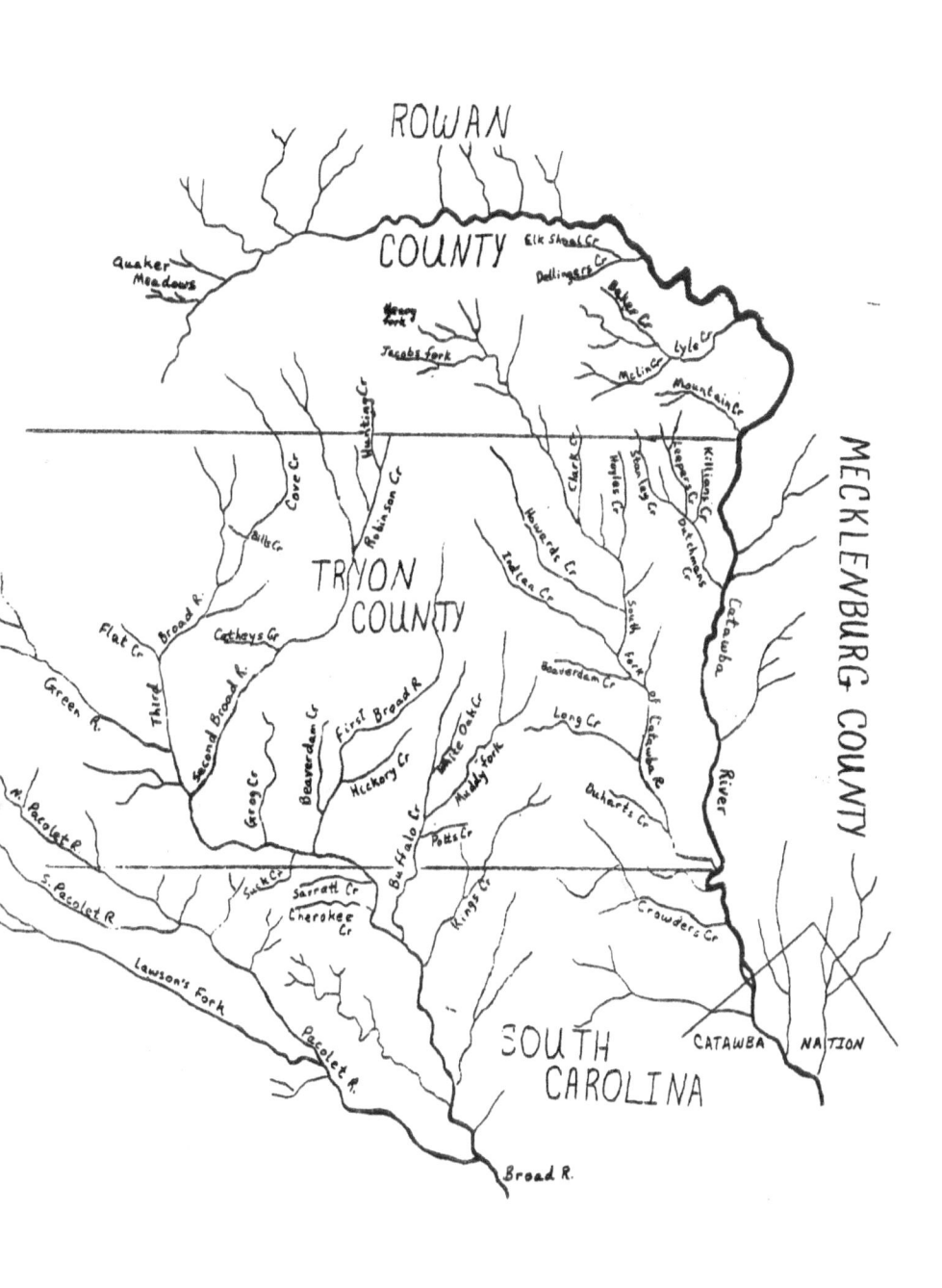

Tryon County, NC Land Entries 1778-1779

Tryon/Lincoln Co, NC land entries 1778-1780 (filed under Rutherford Co CR 086.404.1). Every page is numbered.

page 1 Old First Register of All Land Claims of Record to the time this county was created 1778-1780.

page 3 Book of Land Claims Tryon Co, NC Jan. 22, 1779 Jas Lozar(?).

page 5
1. granted. David Miller claims 200 (? ink blob) ac in Tryon Co on Popular Br of Crowders Cr near the "little Catawba Mountain"; border: Alexander Robinson and his own land; entered Jan. 26, 1778; [£]16.

2. caveated by John Kalliak Apr. 26, 1778; granted to Jas Beard by order of Mar. 22, 1780. James Beard claims 200 ac in Tryon Cr on waters of Little Cataba Cr; border: Abraham Allexandr, Nathaniel Henderson, Hugh Berry, & James Duhart's Mountain; entered Jan. 26, 1778; [£]16.40.

3. granted. William Starret claims 200 ac in Tryon Co on S fork of Cataba R on N side of river; border: Jas Henderson, George Lamkin, & his own land; entered Jan. 26, 1778; £6.4.

4. granted. Nathaniel Alderidge claims 100 ac on branch of Crowders Cr; border: land formerly belonging to James Scott and his own land; entered Jan. 26, 1778; £3 (page torn).

5. granted. Nathaniel Alderidge claims 200 ac in Tryon Co on Falls Br of Crowders Cr; above "said" Falls land on S side of said branch; entered Jan. 26, 1778.

page 6.
6. granted. James Hillhouse claims 100 (? write over) ac in Tryon Co on both sides of Long Cr; border: Carruth, Hoyl, Whittenburg, & his own land; entered Jan. 26, 1778; £3.14.

7. granted. James Hillhouse claims 200 ac in Tryon Co on branch of Long Cr border: Catherine Smith, William Massey, & his own [land]; entered Jan. 26, 1778; £6.4.

8. discontinued by Boston Best. Boston Best jr claims 200 ac on Hoyls Cr; border: John Hoyl, Lewis Lineberger, & his own [land]; entered Jan. 26, 1778; £6.4.

9. granted. John Gillespie claims 100 ac in Tryon Co; border: James Henderson, Frances Gilmore, & his own land; entered Jan. 26, 1778; £3.14.

Tryon County, NC Land Entries 1778-1779

10. granted. Ezekiel Hezlet claims 200 ac in Tryon Co on both sides of a prong of Long Cr; border: Martin Hoyl, Jacob Roads, & William Massey; entered Jan. 26, 1778; £6.4.

page 7
11. granted. Ezikiel Hezlet claims 340 ac in Tryon Co on waters of a prong of Long Cr on Walker Br; border; Joseph Wittenberg, Hoyl, Reed, & John Rudasail; includes his own improvement; entered Jan. 26, 1778; £9,19.

12. granted. Mathew Brown claims 100 (write over) ac in Tryon Co on branch of Little Catawba Cr; border: his own land, John Baird, & William Baird; entered Jan. 26, 1778; £3.14.

13. caveated by George Deal (or Dear); discontinued. Moses Hendry claims 200 ac in Tryon Cr on waters of Crowders Cr; border: his own [land] and David Miller; entered Jan. 26, 1778; £6.4.

14. granted. William Magness claims 100 ac in Tryon Co on Anches Br "Buffalo waters"; border: his own [land] and John Carruth's survey; entered Jan. 26, 1778; £9.14.

15. granted. William Magness claims 150 ac in Tryon Co on waters of Buffalo Cr; border: George Whisinhunt's lower line; entered Jan. 26, 1778; £4.9 (? hole in page).

page 8
16. granted. James Polly claims 108 ac in Tryon Co on branch of Buffeloe Cr; border: George Frout and a "survey than came out formerly in John Sloan's name"; entered Jan. 26, 1778; £3.18.

17. discontinued by James Polly Oct 27, 1778. James Polly claims 300 ac in Tryon Co on waters of Muddy fork a branch of Beaverdam Cr; border: Joseph Dixon and Locust ridge place on N side; entered Jan. 26, 1778; £8.14.

18. granted. Jacob Mony claims 200 ac in Tryon Co on waters of Beaverdam Cr; border: border: Christian Money; includes a road from the court house to Christian (Carpenter ?); entered Jan. 26, 1778; £4.19.

19. granted. Jacob Money claims 150 ac on waters of Beaverdam Cr; border: Christian Money on NW side; includes a path from Christian Money's to widow Caldwell; entered Jan. 26, 1778; £4.19.

20. granted. Allexander Robenson claims 226 (? ink blob) ac in Tryon Cr on waters of Crowders Cr; border: John Robenson, David Miller, & his own land; "being serples land of aforener survey"; entered Jan. 26, 1778; £6.17.

Tryon County, NC Land Entries 1778-1779

page 9
21. granted. John Harris claims 100 ac in Tryon Co on waters of Little Cataba Cr; border: Jonathan Gullicke and his own land; entered Jan. 26, 1778; £3.14.

22. caveated by Cornelis McCarty Apr. 21, 1778; discontinued & money returned Dec. 23(?), 1778; entry given to Cornelius McCarty by law "warrant granted". Jacob Rhine claims 150 ac in Tryon Co on waters of Big Long Cr; border: John Hoyl, Vincent Wiatt, & his own land; entered Jan. 26, 1778; £4.19.

23. granted. Thomas Buchannon claims 100 ac in Tryon Co on waters of Dutchmans Cr; border: William Starret, James Scenter, John Buchannon, & John McKnitt Allexander; entered Jan. 26, 1778; £3.14.

24. granted. John Anderson claims 200 ac in Tryon Co on both sides of Grassey Br of First Broad R; border: John Polk and his own land; entered Jan. 26, 1778; £6.4.

25. granted. John Anderson claims 100 ac in Tryon Co on both sides of Crooked Run of First Broad R; border: John Polk and John Serhoeal; entered Jan. 26, 1778; £3.14.

page 10
26. granted. Benjamen Orman claims 100 ac in Tryon Co on Long Cr and Crowders Cr "waters"; border: James Orman on S side of "his" survey; entered Jan. 27, 1778; £6.4.

27. granted. Benjamin Orman claims 200 ac in Tryon Co on both sides of Long Cr; "being that branch that Thos Espy's saw mill is built on" and above the waggon road; entered Jan. 27, 1778; £6.4.

28. granted. Robert Ferguson claims 100 ac in Tryon Co on waters of Long Cr; border: John Hosteller, Moses Ferguson, & his own land; entered Jan. 27, 1778; £3.14.

29. entered by Moses Hendry; warrant issued to George Pea "if continued". George Pea claims 200 ac in Tryon Co on waters of Crowders Cr on Bare (? ink blob) Br; border: Moses Hendrey, Ambrose Foster, & John Hendrey; includes his improvement; entered Jan. 27, 1778; £6.4.

30. (blank) John McFarland claims 100 ac in Tryon Co on waters of Falls Br; includes Walker's (?) old road between the heads of two branches; entered Jan. 27, 1778; £3.14.

page 11
31. granted. Adam Hostaller claims 200 ac in Tryon Co on waters of Kings Cr; border: Fawning's survey "lower down than Fawning land" upon a branch; entered Jan. 27, 1778; £6.4.

Tryon County, NC Land Entries 1778-1779

32. (caveated by Hugh Jenkins Apr. 23, 1778; this caveat discontinued--all lined out); this entry not to be corrected further Apr. 23, 1778. Ambrose Cobb claims 200 ac in Tryon Co on both sides of Dutchmans Cr on Caney (?) Br; border: Samuel Johnson, Hugh Jenkins, etc; entered Jan. 27, 1778; £6.4.

33. caveated by John Ensly Apr. 21, 1778; this caveat given up by Jno Ensly; warrent granted. Andrew Hezlep claims 200 ac in Tryon Cr on both sides of Buffeloe Cr; border: Samuel Biggerstaff survey on lower side of said survey; includes a shoal on said creek; entered Jan. 27, 1778; £6.4.

34. caveated by John Ensley Apr. 21, 1778; warrent granted; this caveat not to be corrected further Apr. 24, 1778. John Ensley (Andrew Hezlep--lined out) claims 200 ac in Tryon Co on both sides of Buffeloe Cr; border: John Carson; above "said" survey on said creek; entered Jan. 27, 1778; £6.4.

35. caveated by Jas Miller & Jas Logan Feb. 11, 1778; warrent granted to Miller; discoantinued by McCarroll. (following lined out) Nathaniel McCarroll claims 200 ac in Tryon Co on both sides of Pacolet R; above Spriggs improvement; entered Jan. 27, 1778.

page 12
36. caveated by Jas Miller & Jas Logan Feb. 11, 1778; warrent granted to Jas Logan by bargin with Miller; this entry discontinued by McCarrol. (following lined out) Nathaniel McCarrol claims 200 ac in Tryon Co on both sides of N Pacolet R; below his other entry on said river; includes Sprigs improvement; entered Jan. 28, 1778; £6.4.

37. granted. George Horton claims 200 ac in Tryon Co on waters of Big Long Cr; border: Lewis Lineberger, Thomas Hawkens, etc; entered Jan. 28, 1778; £6.4.

38. granted. John Weathers claims 200 ac in Tryon Co on waters of Big and Little Long Creeks; border: Wm Alston and Jacob Rhods; near John Hops (? ink blob) on both sides of road from Spencer's ford to Tryon Court House; entered Jan. 28, 1778; £6.4.

39. granted. Charles Frenderwick Glants (or Slants) claims 700 ac (or 400 ac--write over) in Tryon Co on head of Andrews Br; border: Jacob Glants (or Slants, Conrod Feindergerrard (or Tender Gerrard), Vanzant, and John Dudderod (or Dudder own) survey; includes his own improvement; entered Jan. 28, 1778; £11.4.

40. granted. Andrew Ferguson claims 200 ac in Tryon Co on waters of Crowders Cr; border: William Stenson; above Stenson's land on said creek; entered Jan. 28, 1778; £6.4.

Tryon County, NC Land Entries 1778-1779

page 13

41. James Patterson claims 150 ac in Tryon Cr on waters of Crowders Cr; border: his own land on a large branch running near the said Patterson's old field near William (Masons?); entered Jan. 28, 1778; £4.19.

42. granted. John Hagins (? ink blob) sr claims 200 ac in Tryon Co on both sides of Little Cataba Cr; border: John Beard, (Adamey?) Beard, & John Haggins jr; includes his own improvement; entered Jan. 29, 1778; £6.4.

43. granted. James Henderson claims 224 ac (200--lined out) in Tryon Co on waters of S fork of Cataba R; border: Thomas Hendry, John McClure, George Lamkin, & his own land; entered Jan. 29, 1778; £8.16.

44. caveated by Hugh Jenkins Apr. 23, 1778; caveat given up by Hugh Jenkins "his" own warrent granted. John Rutledge claims 300 (? ink blob) ac in Tryon Co on both sides of Dutchmans Cr; border: George Rutledge, James Coborn(?), James Graham, Hugh Jenkins, & Thomas Ghant; includes his own improvement; entered Jan. 29, 1778; £8.14.

45. granted. Robert Wire claims 100 ac in Tryon Co on Buffeloe Cr; border: John Roan, John Carruth, & his own land; entered Jan. 29, 1778; £3.14.

page 14

46. granted. John Wire (hole in page) ac in Tryon Co on waters of Buffeloe Cr on Murphey (road?); border: Wire and Joseph Glding; enterd Jan. 29, 1778; £4.19.

47. granted. Thomas Espey claims 100 (? ink blob) ac in Tryon Co on waters of Crowders Cr; known as the Big Meadows; entered Jan. 29, 1778; £3.14.

48. granted. Jesse (or Pope) Johnson claims 100 ac on S side of S fork of Catawba R; border: Joe Baird; includes ford in said river known as Armstrong's ford; entered Jan. 29, 1778; £3.14.

49. caveated by Andrew Patrick; entry discontinued & money paid back. Isaac Holland claims 100 ac in Tryon Co on both sides of Little Cataba Cr; border: John Gullick (Saruc?) and his own land; entered Jan. 29, 1778; £3.14.

50. granted. John McClure claims 100 ac in Tryon Cr near main Broad R; border: John McClure, James Miller, & Joseph Kilpatrick; entered Jan. 29, 1778; £3.14.

page 15

51. granted. William Chronicle claims 100 ac in Tryon Co on waters of S fork of Cataba R; border: Abraham Scott, James Cuningham, & Thomas Robison;

Tryon County, NC Land Entries 1778-1779

entered Jan. 29, 1778; £3.14.

52. (caveated by Alexr Coulter Apr. 21, 1778--lined out); "to be caried through & patent brought out". John McClure claims 200 ac in Tryon Co on main Broad R; border: John McClure, Allexander Coulter, & Joseph More; entered Jan. 29, 1778; (£3.14--lined out).

53. granted. Thomas Hendry claims 100 ac in Tryon Co on waters of S fork of Cataba R and on N side of said river; border: James Cunningham, Thomas Robinson, John McClure, & his own land; entered Jan. 30, 1778; £3.14.

54. granted. William Berry claims 100 ac in Tryon Co on waters of Little Cataba and Mill Creeks; border: John Brison, John Balshos, & his own land; entered Jan. 30, 1778; £3.14.

55. granted. Joseph Neil claims 110 ac on waters of Mill Cr; border: James Lewis, (Gerry?), (Frances?) Camphil, Saml Lofton, & (faint); entered Feb. 2, 1778; £3.14.

page 16
56. granted. James Huggins claims 100 ac in Tryon Co on Pots Br of Buffeloe Cr; border: Solomon Beson and his own land; entered Feb. 3, 1778; £3.14.

57. discontinued. (following lined out) Philip Hein claims 200 ac in Tryon Co on waters of Long Cr on Welches Br; border: Thomas Welch and John Hostatler; entered Feb. 3, 1778; £3.14.

58. granted. John Sloan claims 150 (? ink blob) ac in Tryon Co on both sides of Muddy fork of Buffeloe Cr; border: Jacob Money, Gillespie, etc; entered Feb. 3, 1778; £3.14.

59. caveated by John Beard jr Apr. 20, 1778; patented to be "wrought" in John Beard's name; granted. John Beard jr (Huggins--lined out) claims 100 ac in Tryon Co on waters of Long Cr and Little Cataba Cr; includes the ridge road; entered Feb. 3, 1778; £3.14.

60. granted. Joseph Shannon claims 150 ac on waters of Dunharts Cr; border: James Wallace, John Beard, & his own land; entered Feb. 3, 1778; £4.19.

page 17
61. granted. Joseph Hain claims 200 ac in Tryon Co on waters of Buffeloe Cr on Pots Cr; border: James Huggins and Jonathan Pots; includes the great meadows on both sides of the creek; entered Feb. 3, 1778; £6.4.

62. granted. John Sloan claims 200 ac in Tryon Co on waters of Big Hicory (or Huory) Cr; border: Francis & Wallace Boaty and Perygren Magness sr; includes Pery Green Magness jr's improvement; entered Feb. 3, 1778; £6.4.

Tryon County, NC Land Entries 1778-1779

63. granted. John Sloan claims 200 ac in Tryon Co on waters of Muddy fork of Buffeloe and Long Creeks; border: land James Taylor lived on and George Trout; includes Warrick Woodward's improvement; entered Feb. 3, 1778; £6.4.

64. granted to Hugh Berry. Samuel Caldwell (John Huggins--lined out) claims 100 ac in Tryon Co below mouth of Duharts Cr on S fork of Catawba R; border: Hugh Bary (or Bory) "below his land"; entered Feb. 3, 1778; £3.14.

65. claimed by Isaac Holland 100 ac; warrant granted Patrick. Andrew Patrick claims 250 ac in Tryon Co on waters of Little Cataba Cr on both sides of said creek; border: Robert Findley, Allexander Patterson, Jonathan Gullick, & Isaac Holland; includes his own improvement; entered Feb. 5, 1778; £7.9.

page 18
66. granted. Jacob Money claims 100 ac in Tryon Co on waters of S fork of Cataba R on both sides of a large branch; border: Peter Mostiller and Meal Williams; "higher up the branch than Mostiller's land"; entered Feb. 5, 1778; £3.14.

67. caveated by Joseph Glading; given up by Magness; this entry discontinued Oct. 22, 1798. Perry Green Magness jr claims 100(?) ac in Tryon Co on head of Marphego Br of Buffeloe Cr and Frelands Br of said waters; border: Glading and John Wear; entered Feb. 9, 1778; £4.19.

68. granted. Robert Curruth claims 100 ac in Tryon Co on Pilsemmon Br of Buffeloe Cr; border: his own land; entered Feb. 9, 1778; £3.14.

69. granted. Robert Wear claims 100 ac in Tryon Co on both sides of Buffeloe Cr; border: Joseph Glading and his own land; entered Feb. 9, 1778; £3.14.

70. granted. John Sloan claims 200 ac in Tryon Co on Muddy fork of Buffeloe Cr; border: Joseph Dixon; includes Mosor (or Moses) Moree Licklogs on Locust Ridge Br; entered Feb. 9, 1778; £6.4.

page 19
71. granted. Adam Neil claims 100 ac in Tryon Co on waters of Buffeloe Cr; border: his own land; entered Feb. 9, 1778; £3.14.

72. granted to Thomas Fastece. Aaron Rylies claims 100 ac in Tryon Co on S side of Green R; border: begins at upper end of Bottom and "runs down the river"; includes his own improvement "which he bought of Oliver Sutton"; entered Feb. 9, 1778; £3.14.

73. granted. Aaron Reilies claims 200 ac in Tryon Co on waters of Silver Cr on Green R; includes where he lived; entered Feb. 9, 1778; £6.4.

Tryon County, NC Land Entries 1778-1779

74. granted. Deborah Beaty, in behalf of an orphan (for whom she is administrix) named Frances Beaty, claims 100 ac in Tryon Co on waters of Muddy fork of Buffeloe Cr; border: George Trout and Warrich Woodward; entered Feb. 9, 1778; £3.14.

75. granted. Moses Bridges claims 70 (or 40) ac in Tryon Co near mouth of Little Broad R; border: Stephen Shilton (or Shitton) and his own land; entered Feb. 9, 1778; £3.14.

page 20
76. granted. James Sloan claims 100 ac in Tryon Co on Buffeloe Cr; includes his own improvement; border: John Carruth and Anches (hole in page); entered Feb. 9, 1778; £3.14.

77. granted. John Collins claims 100 ac in Tryon Co on waters of Little Hicory Cr "on the main branch"; border: above Benjamin Harding; includes his own improvement; entered Feb. 9, 1778; £3.14.

78. granted. Benjamin Bridges claims 400 ac in Tryon Cr on Little Shoal Cr of First Broad R; border: Jno McKnit Allexander; includes his own improvement; entered Feb. 9, 1778; £11.4.

79. entered by Perry Green Magnes jr. Joseph Glading claims 150 ac in Tryon Co on waters of Buffeloe Cr; border: Walter Jones and his own land; includes his own improvement; entered Feb. 9, 1778; £4.11.

80. granted. Perry Green Magness sr claims 100 ac in Tryon Co on waters of First Broad R; includes a large meadows; entered Feb. 9, 1778; £3.14.

page 21
81. granted. Perry Green Magness sr claims 100 ac in Tryon Co on waters of Big Hicory Cr; border: his upper line; entered Feb. 9, 1778; £3.14.

82. granted. Abel Beaty claims 50 (100--lined out) ac in Tryon Co on both sides of Beaverdam Cr; border: Thomas Beaty and his own land on Cataba R; entered Feb. 9, 1778; £2.0 (3.14--lined out).

83. this warrent to be granted in Aaron Reiley's name; granted. Edward Hampton claims 100 ac in Tryon Co on Camp Br of Bufeloe Cr; border: Jno Wire on both sides of Buffeloe Cr; entered Feb. 9, 1778; £3.14.

84. this warrent to be granted to Geo Cockburn; granted. Abraham Clark claims 200 ac in Tryon Co on waters of Besons Cr; border: Wm Morison and widow Collins; includes a shoal next to Morrison's claims; entered Feb. 9, 1778; £6.4.

85. warrent granted to Davis. John Baptist Davis (Perry Green Magness sr--lined

Tryon County, NC Land Entries 1778-1779

out) claims 900 (? ink blob) ac in Tryon Co on waters of Buffeloe Cr and Big (? ink blob) on head of Anches Branches; border: Grydec on both sides of waggon road; entered Feb. 9, 1778; £6.4.

page 22
86. granted. John Magness claims 150 ac in Tryon Co on main waters of Big Hicory Cr; border: Perry Green Magness and Martin Gryder; entered Feb. 9, 1778; £4.19.

87. granted. Robert Wire claims 200 ac in Tryon Co on waters of Buffeloe Cr; includes Long Br of Magness Cr and George Trout jr's improvement; entered Feb. 9, 1778; £6.4.

88. granted. Perry Green Magness jr claims 100 ac in Tryon Co on Wilkeys Cr of First Broad R; known as Round Meadows; entered Feb. 9, 1778; £3.14.

89. granted. John Huggins jr claims 250 ac in Tryon Co on waters of Wilkies Cr or Beaverdam Cr on largest fork of "said" creek; includes George Bathley's improvement; entered Feb. 10, 1778; £7.8.

90. granted. John Huggins claims 250 ac in Tryon Co on waters of Wilkies Cr; border: John Richmond; includes James Bradley's improvement; entered Feb. 10, 1778; £7.9.

page 23
91. granted. William Gilbert claims 300 ac in Tryon Co; includes fork of Sheppords Cr; border: his own land; entered Feb. 11, 1778; £3.14.

92. entered by Nathaniel McCarrol Jan. 27, 1778; granted to Miller. James Miller claims 200 ac in Tryon Co on waters of N Pacolet R; includes Priggs (or Biggs) improvement "running down to the Ike wuke(?)"; entered Feb. 11, 1778; £6.4.

93. caveated by Phillip Goodbread 200 ac Mar. 7, 1778; granted. Jas Miller claims 400 ac in Tryon Co on both sides of Cove Cr; border: Phillip Goodbread; entered Feb. 11, 1778; £11.4; granted to James Miller by order of court 250 ac of this entry Apr. 14 (or 17), 1788(?).

93A. (blank) Phillip Goodbread claims 200 ac in Tryon Co on both sides of Cove Cr; part of Jas Miller's entry Mar. 9, 1778.

94. granted. Thomas Spriggs claims 100 ac on both sides of N Pacolet R; includes mouth of Vawns Cr; entered Feb. 11, 1778; £3.14.

95A. discontinued. (following lined out) Aron Reily claims (? ink blob) ac in Tryon Co on (ink blob) of Green R; includes the (ink blob) in the upper cove of

Tryon County, NC Land Entries 1778-1779

Green R.

95. entry to be patened in Jas Logan's name; granted. Jas Logan and Jas Miller claims 200 ac in Tryon Co on N Pacolet R; below "his other entry"; includes Spriggs' improvement; entered Feb. 11, 1778; £6.4.

96. granted; discontinued Oct. 2, 1779. Thomas Morris claims 100 ac in Tryon Co on both sides of Chalk hill Cr of Cove Cr; border: mouth of creek; entered Feb. 11, 1778; £3.14.

97. granted. Thomas Spriggs claims 110 ac in Tryon Co on N Pacolet R; known as Little Cain Cr "on both sides of river"; entered Feb. 11, 1778; £3.14.

98. granted. Thomas Whitesides claims 100 ac in Tryon Co on both sides of main Broad R; below Twitty (or Tesitty) land; entered Feb. 11, 1778; £3.14.

99. granted. Henry Kelly claims 100 ac in Tryon Co on both sides of main Broad R below the fork of the "North River"; "fornenst Rugsel land" opposite side of the river; entered Feb. 11, 1778; £3.14.

100. granted. Anthony Dicky claims 400 ac in Tryon Co on Mill Cr on Broad R; border: his own land; entered Feb. 11, 1778; £11.4.

101. [not in book; skip in numbers.]

page 25
102. caveated by James Stacy Feb. 17, 1778; granted to Huddelstone. William Huddelstone claims 100 ac in Tryon Co on waters of Kain Cr; border: James Huen's entry and his own land; entered Feb. 11, 1778; £3.14.

103. entry is patented land & not to be carried any farther May 23, 1778. James Miller claims 100 ac in Tryon Co on Grays Cr of Broad R; "known by Young's old claim" above William Gray's improvement "running up said creek"; entered Feb. 11, 1778; £3.14.

104. granted. Samuel French claims 100 ac in Tryon Co on S side of Green R; border: Samuel French sr "and running up the river"; entered Feb. 11, 1778; £3.14.

105. granted. William Eve claims 100 ac in Tryon Co on Mountain Cr; border: Andrew Hampton; includes the muster grounds and (ink blob); entered Feb. 11, [1778].

106. patented in Robert Melone's name. Thomas Morris claims (ink blob) ac in Tryon Co on both sides of Catheys Cr; border: Wm Gilbert and Bar; entered Feb. 11, 1778; £3.(page torn).

Tryon County, NC Land Entries 1778-1779

page 26

107. granted to Jno Potts by order of Morris Oct. 30, 1779. Thomas Morris claims 100 ac in Tryon Co on Youngs Cr a fork of Cedar Cr; border: George Winters upper line on said creek; entered Feb. 11, 1778; £3.14.

108. granted. Allexander Mackey claims 150 ac in Tryon Co on Horse Cr of (Silver Cr--lined out) N Pacolet R; includes Howard's improvement; entered Feb. 11, 1778; £4.19.

109. caveated by Saml Spencer Mar. 14, 1778; discontinued by Miller & Gilbert Jul. 1, 1778. James Miller and Wm Gilbert claim 480 (or 400) ac in Tryon Co at lower end of lower cover of Green R and "running up"; entered Feb. 11, 1778; £11.4.

190A. (blank) Saml Spencer claims 600 ac in Tryon Co on Little Cove of Green R on both sides of river; entered Mar. 14, 1778.

110. caveated by Saml Spencer Mar (ink blob). William Gilbert and James Miller calim 480 ac at "upper end of their first entry" on Green R "for a complement in the lower cove"; entered Feb. 11, 1778; £12.9.

110A. (blank) Saml Spencer claims 200 ac in Tryon Co on N side of Green R in Little Cove; border: Saml Spencer's 600 ac; entered Mar. 14, 1778.

111. granted. James Largent claims 100 ac in Tryon Co on McGaire Br of Mountain Cr waters of Broad R; includes John Goff's improvement above Marganes land; entered Feb. 11, 1778; £3.14.

page 27

112. granted. John Sorrels claims 200 ac in Tryon Co on Reedy Br of Mountain Cr; above George Winters; includes his own improvement; entered Feb. 12, 1778; £6.4.

113. granted. Thomas Burnet claims 100 ac in Tryon Co on head of Camp Br of Catheys Cr; entered Feb. 12, 1778; £3.14.

114. granted. Thomas Burnet claims 100 ac in Tryon Co on a small branch on S side of Second Broad R; border: McCashland "below said land"; entered Feb. 12, 1778; £3.14.

115. granted. Joseph Burnet claims 150 ac in Tryon Co; border: Thomas Robinson; includes Burrel Sims' improvement; entered Feb. 12, 1778; £4.19.

116. discontinued & money returned Dec. 3, 1778. Robert Melone claims 100 (? ink blob) ac in Tryon Co on (ink blob) of Catheys Cr; border: above George

Tryon County, NC Land Entries 1778-1779

Winters "lower down than Winters' land"; entered Feb. 12, 1778; £3.14.

page 28
117. granted. George Dicky claims 100 ac in Tryon Co on main Broad R; border: North line of Jno McClane's survey and his own land; entered Feb. 12, 1778; £3.14.

118. granted. Giles Williams claims 100 ac in Tryon Co on both sides of main Broad R; between William Nettles and William Robins; entered Feb. 12, 1778; £3.14.

119. granted. Allexander McDonald claims 100 ac in Tryon Co on both sides of Cove Cr; encloses the Cane Break; border: his own land; entered Feb. 12, 1778; £3.14.
120. warrent granted in Joseph Measonatt's(?) name. David Dickey claims 400 ac in Tryon Co on both sides of Green R; border: Whitesides's line "below" and running up the river; entered Feb. 12, 1778; £11.4.

121. granted. John Wood claims 100 ac in Tryon Co on Greens Cr of Whiteoak Cr; border: above his own [land]; entered Feb. 12, 1778; £3.14.

page 29
122. granted. John McKinney claims 79 (written over 100) ac in Tryon Co on N side of main Broad R; on Gilbert's waggon road where it crosses the river; includes Aaron Riely's improvement; entered Feb. 12, 1778; £3.3.6.

123. granted. John Sullins (write over) claims 400 ac in Tryon Co on waters of Little Broad R; includes the high shoal path and Jeremiah Well's improvement; entered Feb. 12, 1778; £11.4.

124. granted. Richard Singleton claims 150 ac in Tryon Co on South Creek of First Broad R; border: Jno Kenconnel's survey and his own land; entered Feb. 13, 1778; £4.19.

125. granted; warrent to be granted James Irving. Richard Singleton claims 100 ac in Tryon Co on Buck Cr of First Broad R; includes his own improvement; entered Feb. 13, 1778; £3.14.

126. granted. Richard Singleton claims 100 ac in Tryon Co on Cherokee Br of Danebar(?) Cr waters of First Broad R; entered Feb. 13, 1778; £3.14.

page 30
127. granted. James Whitesides claims 100 ac in Tryon Co on First Broad R; border: Moses More, William Whitesides, & his own land; entered Feb. 13, 1778; £3.14.

Tryon County, NC Land Entries 1778-1779

128. granted. James Whitesides claims 200 ac in Tryon Co on waters of First Broad R; border: William Whiteside "on the North" and his own land; entered Feb. 13, 1778; £6.4.

129. granted. James Whiteside claims 150 ac in Tryon Co on Beaverdam Cr of First Broad R; includes his own improvement; entered Feb. 13, 1778; £4.19.

130. granted. John Sloan claims 200 ac in Tryon Co on waters of Cove Cr at the forks of Ds (or Do) Cants Br; border: John Potes; entered Feb. 14, 1778; £6.4.

131. granted. Thomas McCormick claims 200 ac in Tryon Co on waters of Shekils Cr; border: John Shekil "on South side" and Yohard; entered Feb. 16, 1778; £6.4.

page 31
132. granted. Thomas McCormick claims 100 ac in Tryon Co on waters of Shekils Cr; border: Soloman Hover and Yohard; entered Feb. 16, 1778; £3.14.

133. granted; entry discontinued & money paid back. John Taylor claims 100 ac in Tryon Co on waters of S fork of Cataba R; border: Wm More, Jno More, & his own land; entered Feb. 16, 1778; £3.14.

134. granted. William Armstrong jr (John Huggins--lined out) claims 250 ac in Tryon Co on Uleys Br; border: John Dudderow and Frederwick Hambright; includes Wm Armstrong jr's improvement; entered Feb. 16, 1778; £7.9.

135. entered by Wm Huddlestone; discontinued by Huey. James Huey claims 100 ac in Tryon Co on waters of Cain Cr; border: John Keithrow and Wm Huddleston; entered Feb. 17, 1778; £3.14.

136. granted. William Hamilton claims 150 ac in Tryon Co on S fork of Cataba R; border: Zacorah Spencer, John Shrimshire(?), John More, & his own land; includes Matthew Pate's improvement; entered Feb. 18, 1778; £(page torn).

page 32
137. granted. James Hollan(?) claims 100 ac in Tryon Co on waters of Beaverdam Cr; border: Chrisly Money on road from court house to Moses More's; entered Feb. 24, 1778; £3.14 [faint entry].

138. granted. John Goodbread claims 150 ac in Tryon Co on main Cove Cr; includes mouth of first creek below Phillip Goodbread's claim; includes his own improvement; entered Feb. 25, 1778; £4.19.

139. granted. John Huggins claims 200 ac in Tryon Co on head waters of Long Cr; border: John Huggins; entered Mar. 5, 1778; £6.4.

Tryon County, NC Land Entries 1778-1779

140. granted. Robt Allison claims 200 ac in Tryon Co on N fork of Crowders Cr; above Charles McLean; includes mouth of Mine Br "and downwards"; entered Mar. 9, 1778; £6.4.

141. granted. Thomas Rowland claims 200 ac in Tryon Co on main Broad R; border: David Lewis' upper corner; includes John Little's improvement; entered Mar. 10, 1778; £6.4.

page 36
142. granted. Allexander Mackey claims 100 ac in Tryon Co on both sides of a creek that runs into Green R at Wm Mills "on S side of river"; entered Mar. 10, 1778; £3.14.

143. granted. Allexdr Mackey claims 200 ac in Tryon Co on Wheats Cr; border: a shoals above David Lewis' improvement; includes Abraham Muzick's three improvements; entered Mar. 10, 1778; £6.4.

144. granted. Jonas Bedford (John Young--lined out) claims 100 ac in Tryon Co on Ritchesons Cr; border: Barney King on both sides of creek; entered Mar. 10, 1778; £3.14.

145. granted. Saml Andrew claims 75 (written over 100) ac in Tryon Co on both sides of Cain Cr of Second Broad R; border: Jas Scott and his own land; entered Mar. 10, 1778; £2.6.6.

146. granted. John Logan claims 200 ac in Tryon Co on fork of Byers Cr; border: "the south line"; includes his own improvement; entered Mar. 10, 1778; £6.4.

147. granted. William Smith claims 100 ac in Tryon Co on Camps Br of Buffeloe Cr; includes Benjamen Harding's improvement; entered Mar. 10, 1778; £3.14.

148. granted. Adam Neil claims 100 ac in Tryon Co on Muddy fork of Buffeloe Cr; includes his own land on N side; entered Mar. 10, 1778; £3.14.

149. granted. James White claims 200 ac in Tryon Co on N fork of Long Cr; border: Mical Hostaller, Andrew Neal, & His own land; entered Mar. 10, 1778; £6.4.

150. granted. Samuel Collins claims 100 ac in Tryon Co on waters of Buffeloe Cr; border: James Collins; includes Samuel Collins jr's improvement; entered Mar. 10, 1778; £3.14.

151. granted. Samuel Espey claims 200 ac in Tryon Co on waters of Crowders Cr; border: Charles McLean on the South side; formerly where Jas Smith lived;

Tryon County, NC Land Entries 1778-1779

entered Mar. 10, 1778; £6.4.

page 35
152. granted. William McGowen claims 300 (? ink blob) ac in Tryon Co on waters of main Broad R; border: Townsend on the N side; includes Thomas Hicks improvement; entered Mar. 10, 1778; £8.14.

153. granted. James Holland claims 200 ac in Tryon Co on Muddy fork of Buffeloe Cr or on both sides of Long Br; border: Barnet; entered Mar. 10, 1778; £6.4.

154. granted. Robert Wire claims 200 ac in Tryon Co on Camp Br of Buffeloe Cr above Graham's path; entered Mar. 10, 1778; £6.4.

155. granted. Robert Wire claims 200 ac in Tryon Co on Williams Cr waters of Broad R; border: Bates improvement; entered Mar. 10, 1778; £6.4.

156. granted to Robert Wire. Joseph Glading claims 100 ac in Tryon Co on first spring Br of Buffeloe Cr; border: Paterson and his own land; entered Mar. 10, 1778; £3.14.

page 36
157. granted. George Cathey jr claims 191 (? write over) ac in Tryon Co on S fork of Cataba R; border: Boston Best and Jas Scenter; includes his mill and improvement; entered Mar. 10, 1778; £(8--lined out).14.

158. granted. Frederwick Hambright claims 300 ac in Tryon Co on waters of Big Long Cr; border: Joseph Jenkins, Lewis Lineberger, (C?) Rudasail, & his own land; includes Norton's improvement; entered Mar. 24, 1778; £8.14 (? write over).

159. granted. William Graham claims 150 (200--lined out) ac in Tryon Co on Calf penn Br of Buffeloe Cr; border: his own land; higher up the creek than his first improvement is; entered Mar. 24, 1778; £4.19 (6.4--lined out).

160. granted. John Logan claims 60 (written over 100) ac in Tryon Co on Shoals Cr of Broad R; includes Camp Spring and William Logan's improvement; entered Mar. 24, 1778; £2.7 (writen over 3.14).

161. granted. Anthony Metcaf claims 46 (written over 100) ac in Tryon Co on N side of Green R; border: Edward Hogan "below" and his own land; entered Mar. 31, 1778; £2.7 (3.14--lined out).

page 37
162. granted. Anthony Metcaf claims (page torn) ac in Tryon Co on N side of Green R; border: Ambrose Mills survey and his own land; entered Mar. 31,

Tryon County, NC Land Entries 1778-1779

1778; £2.0.6 (3.14--lined out).

163. granted. Joseph Beaty claims 100 ac in Tryon Co on N side of S fork of Cataba R; border: John Armstrong and John Chittam; entered Apr. 8, 1778; £3.14.

164. granted. James Logan claims 200 ac in Tryon Co near N and S forks of White Oak(?) Cr; entered Apr. 14, 1778; £6.4 [faint entry].

165. not to be carried "aney" farther; to be carried through the office & patent brought out Jun. 29, 1778. James Logan claims 134 (written over 100) ac in Tryon Co above the mouth of White Oak(?) Cr on both sides of N Pacolet R; entered Apr. 14, 1778; £4.11 (written over 3.14) [faint entry].

166. granted. William Graham (written over John Logan) claims 200 ac in Tryon Co about 0.25 miles above a shoal of fork of ashil(?) Cr; border: John Cummins; entered Apr. 14, 1778; £6.4 [faint entry].

page 38
167. granted. George Paris claims 100 ac on Alstons Cr of Green R; includes fork of the creek; entered Apar. 14, 1778; £3.14.

168. granted. George Davis claims 150 ac in Tryon Co above one of forks of White Oak Cr and a little below Tryon Mountain; border: "towards" Hinnis' old place; entered Apr. 14, 1778; £4.19.

169. granted. Pheby Collins, in behalf of an orphan child for whom she is executrix, claims 150 ac in Tryon Co on both sides of Besons Cr; border: above Abraham Clark's entry; to be patented in John Collins' name; entered Apr. 14, 1778; £3.14.

170. granted. Jonathan Hardin claims 100 ac in Tryon Co; border: Wallace Beaty and David Harding; includes vacant land between David Harding, Francis Beaty, & Wallace Beaty; entered Apr. 20, 1778; £3.14.

171. granted. John Sloan claims 200 ac in Tryon Co on Wiliams Cr waters of First Broad R; border: Alexander McIntyre & John Hightower; includes Jonathan Wilson's improvement; entered Apr. 23, 1778; £6.4.

page 39
172. warrent to be granted to Joseph Sladen. John Dover claims 200 ac in Tryon Co on Long Br of Besons Cr; first improved by Henry Davis and includes "his" improvement; entered Apr. 23, 1778; £6.4.

173. granted. Moses Scott claims 200 ac in Tryon Co on waters of Dutchmans Cr; border: Hugh Jenkins, George Rutledge, & his own land; entered Apr. 23,

Tryon County, NC Land Entries 1778-1779

1778; £6.4.

174. granted. Jonathan Harding claims 600 ac in Tryon Co on both sides of Little Hicory Cr; border: James Crow and Morris Roberts; includes his own improvement; entered Apr. 23, 1778; £16.4.

175. granted. Saml Collins claims 100 ac in Tryon Co on McInteres Br of Buffeloe Cr; includes his own improvement; entered Apr. 23, 1778; £3.14.

176. granted. William Morris claims 100 ac in Tryon Co on Besons Cr of Buffeloe Cr; border: below Abraham Clark's entry; includes his own improvement; entered Apr. 23, 1778; £3.14.

page 40
177. caveated by Andrew Neil Jun. 27, 1778; discontinued. Gilbreath Falls claims 325 ac in Tryon Co on ridge between Beaverdam and Long Creeks; border: Mical Hostatler, Andrew Keller, Christian Money, & Christian Carpenter; includes Wm Wray's improvement; where Aaron Redy now lived; purchased by Gilbreath Falls; entered Apr. 23, 1778; £9.6.6.

178. caveated by John Mattocks Jun. 1, 1778; warrent granted to John Mattox. John Mattox (written over Joseph Beaty?) claims 100 ac in Tryon Co on E side of S fork of Cataba R; border: John Chittem, Francis Armstrong, & John Mattocks; entered May 7, 1778; £3.14.

179. granted. Allexdr Gilleland claims 137 (written over 150) ac in Tryon Co on both sides of ridge road between Falls Br and Crowders Cr; includes James Graham's improvement; entered May 15, 1778; £4.11.6.

180. granted. James White claims 119 (200--lined out) ac in Tryon Co on N branches of Long Cr; border: Robert Ferguson, James Taylor, & his own land; entered May 18, 1778; £4.3.6 (6.4--lined out).

181. granted. Joseph Beaty claims 100 ac in Tryon Co on E side of S fork of Cataba R; border: John Chittam, John Armstrong, & Francis Armstrong; entered May 21, 1778; £3.14.

page 41
182. granted Aug. 22, 1778 to George Davis. James Miller claims 100 ac in Tryon Co on Buffeloe Cr waters of S fork of main Broad R; between Wedlocks and his own land "running round two squares of his own land"; entered May 23, 1778; £3.14.

183. granted. Daniel Hogan claims 100 ac in Tryon Co on N fork of Crowders Cr; border: above Robert Allison's entry on both sides of said branch; includes a small Dears Lick; entered Jun. 3, 1778; £3.14.

Tryon County, NC Land Entries 1778-1779

184. granted. Elias Allexandr claims 100 ac in Tryon Co on Floyds Cr of Broad R; above his own land "on said creek running towards" Richard Hicks survey; entered Jun. 11, 1778; £3.14.

185. granted. James Miller claims 200 ac in Tryon Co on Maple Cr; above and joining "my upper place"; entered Jun. 13, 1778; £6.4.

186. granted. John More claims 150 ac in Tryon Co on Hensons Cr of N Pacolet R; border: mouth of a branch on both sides of creek; includes Henson's improvement; entered Jun. 13, 1778; £4.19.

page 41
"return made" reference #186 Aug. 11, 1778.

2nd 186 [186A]. granted. Allexander Couller claims 100 ac in Tryon Co on a fork of Walnut Cr; includes a spring; entered Jun. 13, 1778; £3.14.

page 43
187. granted. John More claims 100 ac in Tryon Co on middle fork of White Oak Cr on both sides of hunting path; entered Jun. 13, 1778; £3.14.

188. granted. John More claims 100 ac in Tryon Co on N side of main Broad R; above Hugh Queen's on opposide side of river; border: along the Buck Shoal below Blackwell's ford on same river; entered Jun. 13, 1778; £3.14.

189. granted to William Henderson. Richard Saunders claims 100 ac in Tryon Co on Jumping Br of Big Long Cr; border: Adam Curruth and his own land; entered Jun. 13, 1778; £3.14.

190. granted. Jeremiah Smith claims 150 ac in Tryon Co on Wolf Trap Br of Big Long Cr; border: Adam Carruth, Frederwick Hambright, & Mical Rudasail; entered Jun. 20, 1778; £4.19.

191. granted. John Curruth claims 200 ac in Tryon Co on Buffeloe Cr; border: his own land on E side of said creek; entered Jun. 21, 1778; £6.4.

page 44
192. granted. Ralph Wilson claims 100 ac in Tryon Co on Glaghorn Cr of main Broad R; border: James Miller jr "higher up than Miller's land"; entered Jun. 28, 1778; £3.14.

193. caveated by Boston Best sr Aug. 10, 1778; granted to Best by order of court Oct. 13, 1778. William McKinsey claims 200 (written over 600) ac in Tryon Co on N side of S fork of Cataba R; includes Benjamin Taylor's improvement; entered Jul. 3, 1778; £6.4.

Tryon County, NC Land Entries 1778-1779

194. granted Nov. 16, 1778. Samuel Spencer claims 400 ac in Tryon Co on both sides of Alstons Cr of Green R; border: a cove on S side of creek about 1.5 miles above Alston and a branch; entered Jul. 8, 1778; £11.4.

195. Charles Medlock caveated 300 ac of Spencer's entry Oct. 21, 1778; caveat discontinued and granted to Spencer. Saml Spencer claims 400 ac in Tryon Co on both sides of upper Buffeloe Cr of Broad R near foot of Bald Mountain; above and border: William Basset's survey, James Bedford, & Saml Spencer's former survey; entered Jul. 8, 1778; £11.4.

196. Aug. 6, 1778 Saml Spencer discontinued entry. Saml Spencer claims 400 ac in Tryon Co on both sides of upper Buffeloe Cr of Broad R; above and border: his other entry; 260 ac of this entry "amt for(?) hundred above his head rights"; entered Jul. 3, 1778; £16.13 (? write over).

page 45
197. granted to Mathew Russell. William Massey claims 200 ac in Tryon Co on waters of Big Long Cr; border: Wm Smith sr, Gray, & his own land; includes Richard Saunders improvement; entered Jul. 17, 1778; £6.4.

198. Sept. 22, 1778 entry not to be caried any farther; discontinued. James Cuningham claims 150 ac in Tryon Co on Cuninghams Cr of Cataba R; border: Thomas Robinson, James Beaty, Saml Elder, & his own land; entered Jul. 18, 1778; £4.19.

199. granted. James Hillhouse claims 200 ac on waters of Big Long Cr; border: his 200 ac entry; includes part of John Pinner's improvement and a large spring near the ridge road; entered Jul. 20, 1778; £6.4.

200. caveated by Saml(?) Spencer Jul. 22, 1778. James Miller and William Gilbert claim 400 ac on lower end of lower cove of Green R; entered Jul. 21, 1778; £11.4.

201. caveated by Saml Spencer Jul. 22, 1778. William Gilbert and Jas Miller claim 450 ac in Tryon Co; "at" upper end of their first entry on Green R in the lower cove; entered Jul. 21, 1778; £11.9(?).

page 46
202. caveated by Ambrose Cobb Aug. 7, 1778; granted to Jenkins by order of court Oct. 13, 1779. Hugh Jenkins claims 400 ac in Tryon Co on both sides of Dutchmans Cr on Caney Br; border: George Rutledge, Saml Johnson, & his own land; entered Jul. 21, 1778; £11.4.

203. granted. Hugh Jenkins calims 100 ac in Tryon Co on Killians Cr; border: Killian, James Jenkins, & his own land; includes a mineral spring; entered Jul.

Tryon County, NC Land Entries 1778-1779

21, 1778; £3.14.

204. discontinued & money paid back Apr. 21, 1779. John Hostatler claims 300 ac in Tryon Co on head branches of Long Cr; border: Thomas Welch "on the N side"; entered Jul. 21, 1778; £8.14.

205. granted. Simon Kirkindal claims 100 ac in Tryon Co on branch of Kings Cr; border: William Sharp and Jacob Connel; includes a shoal; entered Jul. 22, 1778; £3.14.

206. granted. John Scott claims 200 ac in Tryon Co on both sides of Walnut Cr of Green R; border: Jno Phipher desc and Wm Mills survey; entered Jul. 21, 1778; £3.14.

page 47
207. granted. James Scott claims 100 ac in Tryon Co on Walnut Cr of Green R; below Allexdr Coulter; border: said Coulter and Griffith Rutherford; entered Jul. 21, 1778; £3.14.

208. granted. James Linn claims 150 ac in Tryon Co on both sides of Second Broad R; border: Cathey and Nathan Prockter; entered Jul. 21, 1778; £4.19.

209. granted Jan. 29, 1779. Thomas Greans claims 100 ac in Tryon Co on Second Broad R; border: William Bridget and his own land; entered Jul. 22, 1778; £3.14.

210. 100 ac of entry caveated by Thomas Simons Sept. 28, 1778. Stephen Langford claims 200 ac in Tryon Co on Marlins Cr of First Broad R; includes his own improvement; entered Jul. 22, 1778; £6.4.

210A (blank) Thomas Simons claims 100 ac in Tryon Co on Marlins Cr of First Broad R; includes his own improvement; entered Sept. 28, 1778.

211. entry is held by Arnold patent & discontinued & money paid back to Langford Oct. 24, 1778. Stephen Langford claims 200 ac in Tryon Co on both sides of First Broad R; includes the widow's field at first ford above William Willis; entered Jul. 22, 1778; £6.4.

page 48
212. granted. James Rutledge (written over James Logan) claims 150 ac in Tryon Co on waters of Dutchmans Cr; border: Wills and his own land; entered Jul. 22, 1778; £4.19.

213. granted. Jonas Bedford claim 200 ac in Tryon Co on both sides Brier Cr; above Kirkonel's land; entered Jul. 22, 1778; £6.4.

214. granted Jan. 29, 1779. Jonas Bedford claims 150 ac in Tryon Co on both

Tryon County, NC Land Entries 1778-1779

sides of Robisiness Cr (or Hobiesiness); above Bracket's land; entered Jan. 22, 1778; £4.19.

215. granted. Joseph More claims 100 ac in Tryon Co on Walnut Cr of Green R; above William Mills land; entered Jul. 23, 1778; £3.14.

216. granted. David Gage claims 200 ac in Tryon Co on Sandy Run of Broad R; border: Parmers or place where Riggs now lives; includes his own improvement; entered Jul. 23, 1778; £6.4.

page 49
217. granted. William Grahams claims 100 ac in Tryon Co on both sides of N Pacolet R; below the little cane break; entered Jul. 23, 1778; £3.14.

218. caveated by Benjamin Johnson Sept. 22, 1778; granted to Wm Graham by order of court Oct. 13, 1779. William Graham claims 100 ac in Tryon Co on both sides of Buffeloe Cr; border: his upper line; entered Jul. 23, 1778; £3.14.

219. granted. William Hall claims 100 ac in Tryon Co on S side of main Broad R; border: his own land opposite McFadden's house on S side of river; entered Jul. 23, 1778; £3.14.

220. granted. Andrew Hedigh claims 100 ac in Tryon Co on James Cr on S fork of Cataba R; border: Robert McCashland and his own land; entered Jul. 23, 1778; £3.14.

221. granted. John Smith claims 100 ac in Tryon Co on First Broad R; border: William Willis jr and Collenwood; includes a shoal on said river; entered Jul. 24, 1778; £3.14.

page 50
222. granted. Jacob Plank claims 300 ac in Tryon Co on Big Br waters of Big Long Cr; border: Peter Plank, James White, Thomas Espey, & Adam Curruth; includes his own improvement; entered Jul. 25, 1778; £8.14.

223. granted. James Martin claims 100 ac in Tryon Co on E side of Crowders Cr; border: John Hendry, tract were Charles Hamelton now lives, & his own land; entered Jul. 26, 1778; £3.14.

224. caveated by Absalem Gregory Aug. 27, 1778; granted to Gregory. James Magness claims 150 ac in Tryon Co on Little Broad R; includes mouth of Long Br and Gregory's improvement "opposite Tubb's land on other side of the river"; entered Aug. 2, 1778; £4.19.

225. caveated by Jonathan Fouch Aug. 27, 1778; caveat discontinued Magness gives up claim to Fouch Oct. 21, 1778; granted to Fouch Feb. 23, 1778. Perry

Tryon County, NC Land Entries 1778-1779

Green Magness jr claims 150 (written over 100) ac in Tryon Co on E side of Little Broad R; border: Pipe; includes Jonathan Fouk's improvement; entered Aug. 2, 1778; £4.19.

226. granted. John Hoyl claims 100 ac in Tryon Co on ridge path between Long Cr and the South fork River; border: his own land; entered Aug. 2, 1778; £3.14.

page 51
227. granted. Denis Duff claims 100 ac in Tryon Co on Durnalds Cr of Cove Cr; includes the little came break; border: mouth of Plant Br; entered Aug. 2, 1778; £3.14.

228. granted. Saml Spencer claims 200 ac in Tryon Co on upper Skilwicker Br of N Pacolet R; border: oak tree about 0.5 mile from mouth of branch; entered Aug. 6, 1778; £6.4.

229. granted. Saml Spencer claims 300 ac in Tryon Co on N fork of White Oak Cr; border: border: about 0.25 [mile?] below John Nicoloas Folly; entered Aug. 6, 1778; £8.14.

230. granted to Roler (or Roter) Wire. James Holland and Robert Wire claim 200 ac in Tryon Co on W side of First Broad R on mouth of George Harris Br; border: Harris and Thomas Arrington; includes Absolem Otries (or Ortries) improvement; entered Aug. 8, 1778; £6.4.

231. granted by agreement to Robert Holaway. Jas Holland claims 200 ac in Tryon Co on W side of First Broad R above waggon road from Tryon Court house to Jno Walker; includes William Gardiner improvement; entered Aug. 8, 1778; £6.4.

page 52
232. granted. John Holland claims 200 ac in Tryon Co on both sides of Luck fork of Buffeloe Cr; border: Phineas Clayton on both sides of Broad R from Rillies (or Killies) to Carsons and William Booth; includes Samuel Julian improvement; entered Aug. 8, 1778; £6.4.

233. warrent to be granted to Edward Jenkins May 20, 1779; granted to Jenkins. Jas Wyatt (David Jenkins--lined) claims 200 ac in Tryon Co on S side of Little Long Cr; border: Peter Carpenter; includes "his" house where he now lives and a part of a field running towards the ridge road; entered Aug. 10, 1778; £6.4.

234. granted. Daniel Gray claims 100 ac in Tryon Co on Ried Br waters of Long Cr; border: George (or Geaga) Lampkin, Tray, & his own land; includes John Gorman improvement; entered Aug. 17, 1778; £3.14.

235. granted. Samuel Dunaway claims 400 ac in Tryon Co on N side of Little

Tryon County, NC Land Entries 1778-1779

Long Cr; border: near mouth of Rock Spring Br; border: Little, Jas Wyatt, Peter Carpenter, & Frederwick Glant's entry; includes his own and Thomas Wiatt's improvements; entered Aug. 18, 1788; £11.4.

236. granted. James Sloan claims 100 ac in Tryon Co on waters of Buffeloe Cr; border: John Carruth; entered Aug. 18, 1778; £3.14.

page 53
237. granted. David Thompson claims 300 ac in Tryon Co on W side of First Broad R on Pipes Br; border: William Tubbs and John Moffit; includes his own improvement; entered Aug. 20, 1778; £3.14.

238. granted. John Lusk claims 200 ac in Tryon Co on W side of First Broad R; border: David Thompson's entry; includes small improvement made by David Thompson and place called the Flat Rocks; entered Aug. 20, 1778; £6.4.

239. granted. Robert Wire claims 50 ac in Tryon Co on waters of Potts Cr; surplus land of a former survey; border: Joseph Glading and his own land; this 50 ac above his head rights; entered Aug. 22, 1778; £3.14.

240. granted. John Tucker claims 150 ac in Tryon Co on Beaverdam Br of Dutchmans Cr; border: David Abernathey, Jacob Sides, & Baldridge; entered Aug. 25, 1778; £4.19.

241. granted. John Fergus claims 150 ac in Tryon Co on Long Br of Buffeloe Cr; includes fork of said branch and a large meadow below the fork; entered Aug. 25, 1778; £4.19.

page 54
242. granted. James Mode claims 150 ac in Tryon Co on First Broad R; border: Alexdr McIntire, land where Jonathan Gregory lives, & James Sloan's entry; includes his own improvement; entered Aug. 28, 1778; £4.19.

243. granted to Thomas Campbell by bargin of More. Thomas Campbell (Alexdr More--lined out) claims 200 ac in Tryon Co on waters of Duharts Cr; border: Hugh Shannon and Jos Shannon; on E side of Jos Shannon's land; entered Aug. 29, 1778; £6.4.

244. granted. William McCarter claims 100 ac in Tryon Co on S branches of Crowders Cr or branch called Mill Cr; border: his own land on N side; entered Aug. 29, 1778; £3.14.

245. granted to Zakariah Salaris by order of Smith. Jeremiah Smith claims 200 ac in Tryon Co on both sides of Boreings Cr at First Broad R; border: John McKinney; includes Jno (Iec?) improvement; entered Aug. 20, 1778; £6.4.

Tryon County, NC Land Entries 1778-1779

246. granted. William More jr claims 150 ac in Tryon Co on Lick Br of Duharats Cr; border: John More, Frances Selmon, & His own land; entered Sept. 1, 1778; £4.19.

page 55
247. granted. Jas Bradly claims 100 ac in Tryon Co on S side of Little Broad R; border: John Lusk; entered Sept. 1, 1778; £3.14.

248. granted; discontinued May 20, 1779; carried through in John Holland's name. Thomas Henderson claims 150 ac in Tryon Co on Logans Br of Little Cataba Cr; includes fork of said branch; above Logan's land where path crosses that leads to Major Hambright's; entered Sept. 7, 1778; £4.19.

249. granted; discontinued money returney. Jno McKnight Allexander claims 300 ac in Tryon Co on Floyds Cr; near 2 miles above Elias Allexander's and nearly including Richard Barry's survey; entered Sept. 12, 1778; £8.14.

250. granted. Jonas Bedford claims 100 ac in Tryon Co on South Cr of First Broad R "on left hand fork of on Coals Mountain"; entered Sept. 11, 1778; £3.14.

251. granted. Jonas Bedford claims 150 ac in Tryon Co on right hand fork of Duncans Cr of First Broad R; above punkin Roost near Lively's land; entered Sept. 11, 1778; £3.14.

252. granted. Jonas Bedford claims 100 ac in Tryon Co on Upper Buffeloe Cr of main Broad R; about 1 mile above his own land above the Rock House Bottom; entered Sept. 11, 1778; £3.14.

253. granted. Jonas Bedford claims 100 ac in Tryon Co on head of Walnut Cr of Green R; entered Sept. 11, 1778; £3.14.

254. granted. Jonas Bedford claims 100 ac in Tryon Co on left hand fork of Beatys Cr of First Broad R; about 0.5 mile above Stephen Langford's land; entered Sept. 11, 1778; £3.14.

255. granted. Jonas Bedford claims 100 ac in Tryon Co on Duncans Cr of First Broad R; on S side of Lively's Gap about 1 mile above Lively's land; enterd Sept. 11, 1778; £3.14.

256. granted. Jonas Bedford claims 100 ac in Tryon Co on a branch of Duncans Cr of First Broad R; near Lesenbags Mountain; about 1.5 miles from William Whitesides' land; entered Sept. 11, 1778; £3.14.

page 57
257. granted. Jonas Bedford claims 100 ac in Tryon Co on Kyrkonels Br of First

Tryon County, NC Land Entries 1778-1779

Broad R; includes Holy Spring; entered Sept. 11, 1778; £3.14.

258. granted. Jonas Bedford claims 100 ac in Tryon Co on both sides of First Broad R; about 3 miles above John Smith's land; includes "where there was logs cut formerly"; entered Sept. 11, 1778; £3.14.

259. granted. Daniel Wyatt jr claims 100 ac in Tryon Co on N side of S fork of Cataba R; border: Jno McKnight Allexdr, Jas Scenter sr, & his own land; includes his own improvement; entered Sept. 14, 1778; £3.14.

260. granted. Charles McDowell claims 200 ac in Tryon Co; border: on SE George Winters "whereon he now lives" and up both sides of "said" branch; includes a meadow; entered Sept. 18, 1778; £6.4.

261. granted. James Miller jr claims 300 ac in Tryon Co on Kain Cr; border: Miller; entered Sept. 18, 1778; £8.14.

page 58
262. granted. James Miller jr claims 100 ac in Tryon Co on Earricks Cr; border: Twitty on upper side; entered Sept. 18, 1778; £3.14.

263. granted. James Miller jr claims 200 ac in Tryon Co on Flat Br of Broad R; below mouth of Kain Cr; entered Sept. 18, 1778; £6.4.

264. granted. John Lusk claims 100 ac in Tryon Co on E side of Little Broad R; border: his own land; includes a small improvement; entered Sept. 27, 1778; £3.14.

265. granted. David Elder claims 125 ac in Tryon Co on branch of Duharts Cr; border: his own land on S side; entered Sept. 28, 1778; £4.6.

266. granted. George Smith claims 100 ac in Tryon Co on left had fork of Beatys Cr of First Broad R; border: Beaty's land on S side "higher up the creek" on both sides of creek; entered Sept. 28, 1778; £3.14.

page 59
267. granted to Joseph Dickson. Wm Chronicle claims 200 ac in Tryon Co on waters of Kyrkindals Cr; border: Wm More's old line that is now Thos Polk's and land of Joseph Gilbreath; entered Sept. 28, 1778; £6.4.

268. granted; discontinued by Wm Chronicle Spet. 11, 1779. Wm Chronicle claims 100 ac in Tryon Co on Dunkans Cr of First Broad R; border: Lively; includes Drues improvement; entered Sept. 28, 1778; £3.14.

269. granted. William Camp claims 150 ac in Tryon Co on N side of main Broad R; border: Thomas Brothers "partly above & between Brothers land and

Tryon County, NC Land Entries 1778-1779

the river" and "line of the south state"; includes his own improvement; entered Oct. 3, 1778; £5.19.

270. granted. John Fergus claims 300 ac in Tryon Co on Maple Swamp; border: James Wilson; includes ground where Benjamin Harding's company now meets to muster; entered Oct. 3, 1778; £3.14. [note: out of order; in book #271 comes before #270.]

271. granted. Frances Guthery claims 150 a in Tryon Co on branch of Maple Swamp; border: on S side of John Fergus' entry and on both sides of waggon road from Carson's and Harding's; entered Oct. 3, 1778; £4.19.

page 60
272. granted. Phillip Hein claims 300 ac in Tryon Co on Wolfs Br of Muddy fork of Buffeloe Cr; includes John Swil's cabbin; entered Oct. 5, 1778; £8.14.

273. granted. Thomas Hendry claims 40 ac in Tryon Co on N side of branch of S fork of Cataba R; border: Abrahaam Scott, Thos Robinson, & his own land; entered Oct. 6, 1778; £2.4.

274. granted; discontinued & money paid back Aug. 4, 1779. Abel Beaty claims 50 ac in Tryon Co on both sides of Buffeloe Cr; border: William Magness and his own land; entered Oct. 7, 1778; £2.9.

275. granted. Abel Beaty claims 100 ac in Tryon Co on Little Cr "otherwise" Magness Cr of Buffeloe Cr "on both sides of said creek"; border: on N of Robt Barkly; entered Oct. 7, 1778; £3.14.

276. granted to Thos Dickson by Lamkin. George Lampkins jr claims 100 ac in Tryon Co on N side of main branch of Duharts Cr; border: Daniel Gray, James Thomson, & Wallace; includes "where there is house logs cut"; entered Oct. 13, 1778; £3.14.

page 61
277. granted. Hugh Torrance claims 100 ac in Tryon Co on waters of Little Cataba Cr; border: "two squares" of his own land where he now lives on N and NW sides; entered Oct. 16, 1778; £3.14.

278. granted. William Rice claims 200 ac in Tryon Co on waters of Little Cataba Cr; border: Thos Campbel's land "where Jas Aldridge built a cabbin", Thomas Norman, Nathaniel Aldridge, & his own land; enterd Oct. 16, 1778; £6.4.

279. granted. William Rice claims 100 ac in Tryon Co on Little Cr "otherwise" Goforth's Cr of Crowders Cr; border: Allexandr Robinson, John Beard jr, & Violet Tagert; entered Oct. 16, 1778; £3.14.

Tryon County, NC Land Entries 1778-1779

280. discontinued & money returned. David Liles claims 250 ac in Tryon Co on upper fork of Brier Cr of First Broad R; includes a place called the cave (or cowe) above Jonas Bedford's entry #213; entered Oct. 21, 1778; £7.9.

281. granted. Jonas Bedford claims 300 ac in Tryon Co on S side of First Broad R "on both sides of said river"; includes mouth of Brier Cr; entered Oct. 21, 1778; £8.14.

page 62
282. caveated by Henry Duly 100 ac of this entry Oct. 21, 1778; Hendricks gives up & receives his money; discontinued. John Hendricks claims 200 ac in Tryon Co on S side of Green R; includes mouth of Doolys Cr; border: Joseph McDaniel on opposite side of river; entered Oct. 21, 1778; £3.14 (written over 6.4).

283. entered by John Hendricks Oct. 21, 1778. Hendry Duly claims 100 ac in Tryon Co on S side of Green R; border: his land; entered Oct. 22, 1778; £3.14.

284. entered by Saml Spencer Jul. 8(?), 1778; this caveat cannot be caried any farther as the "three marks" is out; discontinued. Charles Medlock claims 100 [ac] in Tryon Co on both sides of upper Buffeloe Cr or main Broad R; above Miller's entry; entered Oct. 21, 1778; money paid back to "Dunn" Apr. 20, 1779.

285. granted. Abraham Kuyrkindall claims 200 ac in Tryon Co on Sandy Run; below waggon road from Collonell Walker's to Charles Town; includes his own improvement where he now lives; entered Oct. 22, 1778; £6.4.

286. granted. Abraham Kuyrkindall claims 100 ac in Tryon Co on both sides Groog (or Sroog) Cr; on both sides of path from his house to Abel Hill's; includes John Turner's cabbin; entered Oct. 22, 1778; £3.14.

page 63
287. granted. Mathew Guthery claims 100 ac in Tryon Co on S side of main Broad R; includes Island fork shoals and his own improvement; entered OCt. 22, 1778; £3.14.

288. granted. Joseph Beaverns claims 100 ac in Tryon Co on Hintons Cr of First Broad R; border: Nicholas Leeper; includes his own improvement; entered Oct. 22, 1778; £3.14.

289. granted. William Suitar claims 100 ac in Tryon Co on N side of Buffeloe Cr; border: James McAfee and his own land; includes where said Suitar cut logs; entered Oct. 22, 1778; £3.14.

290. granted. John Potts claims 100 ac in Tryon Co; includes where he lives and the meeting house; entered Oct. 22, 1778; £3.14.

Tryon County, NC Land Entries 1778-1779

291. granted. John (written over Mary) Potts claims 100 ac in Tryon Co on N fork of Cedar Cr; border: Richard Ledbetter's upper line; entered Oct. 22, 1778; £3.14.

page 64
292. granted. John Collins claims 100 ac in Tryon Co on Little Hicory Cr of First Broad R; border: his other entry on E side; entered Oct. 22, 1778; £3.14.

293. granted. Allexdr Davidson claims 100 ac in Tryon Co on N side of main Broad R; border: "his own land above" on the river; includes Guthery's improvement; entered Oct. 22, 1778; £3.14.

294. granted. Andrew Nelson claims 200 ac in Tryon Co on Hinsons Cr on First Broad R; includes the three forks of said creek and where he now lives; entered Oct. 22, 1778; £6.4.

295. granted. Samuel Hais claims 200 ac in Tryon Co on both sides of Green R; border: Joseph McDaniel and Edward Hogan; entered Oct. 22, 1778; £6.4.

296. granted. Denis Heron claims 100 ac in Tryon Co on N side of main Broad R; includes William Pool's improvement; entered Oct. 22, 1778; £6.4.

page 65
297. granted. Jacob Connel claims 100 ac in Tryon Co on Magness Cr of Buffeloe Cr on both sides of "said" Little Cr; border: Jas Sloan; entered Oct. 22, 1778; £3.14.

298. granted. Benjamin Harding jr claims 100 ac in Tryon Co on Little Hicory Cr of First Broad R; border: David Harding, Morrice Roberts, & John Collins' entry; includes his own improvement; entered Oct. 22, 1778; £3.14.

299. granted. Allexander Coulter claims 100 ac in Tryon Co on both sides of Walnut Cr of Green R; border: above James Scott's entry; includes a shoal and his own improvement; entered Oct. 23, 1778; £3.14.

300. granted. Mary 14. John Jackson More claims 100 ac in Tryon Co on Chism fork of Hintons Cr of First Broad R; includes his own improvement; entered Oct. 23, 1778; £3.14.

301. discontinued Dec. 7, 1778 money paid back. Joseph McDaniel claims 200 ac in Tryon Co on main fork of White Oak Cr "otherwise" Uptons Mill Cr; includes mouth of Glady fork; entered Oct. 23, 1778; £6.4.

page 66
302. granted. Mar. 14. Perry Green Magness jr claims 150 ac in Tryon Co on

Tryon County, NC Land Entries 1778-1779

Brushey Cr of First Broad R; above or joining Swafford's land; includes a shoal on said creek and an old improvement; entered Oct. 23, 1778; £4.19.

303. granted. John Huselbery (or Husdbery) claims 200 ac in Tryon Co on Potts Cr of Buffeloe Cr; border: Soloman Beson on N side; includes his cabbin and improvement; entered Oct. 23, 1778; £6.4.

304. granted. Christopher Walver claims 300 ac in Tryon Co on both sides of Wards Cr; border: Thomas Robinson and Edward Frances; includes forks of the creek and his own improvement; entered Oct. 23, 1778; £8.14.

305. granted. William Porter claims 100 ac in Tryon Co on branch of Camp Cr of Second Broad R; border: his own land on W side; entered Oct. 23, 1778; £3.14.

306. granted Mar. 14. Wiliam Beaty claims 150 ac in Tryon Co on S side of Cataba R; border; Thomas Beaty between his land and Beaty's ford and "up the river around Beaty's ford"; where Abel Beaty formerly lived; entered Oct. 23, 1778; £4.19.

page 67
307. granted. John Carpenter claims 150 ac in Tryon Co on W side of Buffeloe Cr; border: his own land where he now lives; entered Oct. 23, 1778; £4.19.

308. granted. Joseph Camp claims 400 ac in Tryon Co on branch of Wades Mill Cr on E side of main Broad R; border: Joseph Boreing; includes improvement where George Blanton lives; entered Oct. 23, 1778; £11.8.

309. granted. Uel (or W C) Lampkin claims 150 ac in Tryon Co on Nob Cr of First Broad R; includes forks of said creek "otherwise" Benjamin Hardings Mill Cr; border: Joseph Harding and his own land; includes part of his own improvement; entered Oct. 23, 1778; £4.19.

310. discontinued by Jas Logan. James Logan claims 250 ac in Tryon Co on that fork of White Oak Cr where Capshaw mill is built "otherwise" the middle fork; border: White's "below and running down both sides of said creek"; includes Beaverdam meadows; entered Oct. 23, 1778; £7.9.

[310A] granted. James Losan jr claims 50 ac in Tryon Co on Nawns Cr above Skriggs' entry; entered Oct. 23, 1778; £2.9.

311. granted. James Logan claims 200 ac in Tryon Co on both sides of Sandy Run; includes shoal and where Joseph Davis made an improvement; entered Oct. 23, 1778; £6.4.

page 68

Tryon County, NC Land Entries 1778-1779

312. granted. William Davis claims 200 ac in Tryon Co on heads of Duharts Cr; border: William Smith sr, John Beard, Daniel Gray, Wallace, & his own land; includes Joseph Magness cabbin; entered Oct. 31, 1778; £6.4.

313. granted. Robert Miller claims 100 ac in Tryon Co on Big Br of Little Cataba Cr; border: Wm Beard desc, Berry, Thomas Norman, & his own land where he now lives; entered Oct. 31, 1778; £3.14.

314. granted. George Patterson claims 100 ac in Tryon Co on head of Kings Cr; border: Henry Jasper on W side; includes his own improvement. entered Oct. 31, 1778; £3.14.

315. granted. David Ramsey claims 35 ac in Tryon Co on waters of Howards Cr; border: John Bolinger and his own land; includes an old field; entered Oct. 31, 1778; £2.1.6.

316. granted. John Jones claims 250 ac in Tryon Co on Micals Cr on S fork of Cataba R; border: Philip Cancellor, Andrew Heigh, & Jno McKt Allexdr; includes his own improvement; entered Nov. 2, 1778; £7.9.

page 69
317. granted. Saml Aspey claims 100 ac in Tryon Co on Big Meadow Br of Crowders Cr; border: Thomas Espey's entry; entered Nov. 2, 1778; £3.14.

318. granted. Peter Castner claims 200 ac in Tryon Co on S side of Big Long Cr; border: Mical Hoyl, Blackwood, & his own land; entered Nov. 7, 1778; £6.4.

319. granted. John Hoyl claims 200 ac in Tryon Co on S side of S fork of Cataba R; border: his own land "on the S side on his open line"; includes crossing of paths between his house and John Weather's; entered Nov. 10, 1778; £6.4.

320. granted. Moses Scott claims 150 ac in Tryon Co on samll branch that runs into Cataba R; border: David Phillips the river; entered Nov. 10, 1778; £4.19.

321. John Ashley discontinued this entry Jan. 13, 1779. John Ashley claims 100 ac on head of Duharts Cr; border: Milliam Smith jr and James Hillhouse's entry; includes the ridge road; entered Nov. 10, 1778; £3.14.

page 70
322. granted. John Sloan sr claims 300 ac in Tryon Co on N branch of Big Hicory Cr of First Broad R; border: McKinney; includes Jonathan Gregory's improvement; entered Nov. 13, 1778; £3.14.

323. granted. Wallace Beaty claims 150 ac in Tryon Co on N side of Big Hicory Cr; border: his own land on N side; includes path from Magness to Tubbs; entered Nov. 13, 1778; £4.19.

Tryon County, NC Land Entries 1778-1779

324. granted. James Hilhouse claims 50 ac in Tryon Co on Jumping Br of Long Cr; border: Whitenberg, Carruth, & his own land; entered Nov. 16, 1778; £2.9.

325. granted. James Dalley claims 40 ac in Tryon Co on waters of Muddy fork of Buffeloe Cr; border: Deborah Beaty, Neil, & Aaron Reily; entered Nov. 16, 1778; £2.4.

326. granted. Jonathan Gullick claims 200 (? write over) ac in Tryon Co on waters of Locust Ridge Br of Buffeloe Cr; border: Joseph Dixon's survey on E side; entered Nov. 16, 1778; £7.7.

page 71
327. granted. John Fergus claims 100 ac in Tryon Co on Luck fork of Buffeloe Cr; border: Phineas Clayton; includes waggon road from Tuaquers(?) to Soloman Beson and a shoal where road crosses said water course; entered Nov. 18, 1778; £3.14.

328. granted. John Dinnard claims 100 ac in Tryon Co on head of S fork of Nicke Cr on S side of main Broad R; includes his own improvement; entered Nov. 20, 1778; £3.14.

329. granted. Mar. 26. Robert Allexander claims 200 ac in Tryon Co on waters of Groves Br of Crowders Cr; border: John McFarland; entered Nov. 20, 1778; £6.4.

330. granted. Phillip (Robert--lined out) Hein claims 250 ac in Tryon Co near the head of Long Br of Buffeloe Cr on both sides of said branch; includes forks of branch and Wasons old cabbin; entered Nov. 21, 1778; £7.9.

331 granted. William Davis claims 100 ac in Tryon Co on Duharts Cr below his 200 ac entry #312; border: Wallace, Beard, & his own land; entered Nov. 21, 1778; £3.14. [faint entry]

page 72
332. granted. John Huggins jr claims 100 ac in Tryon Co on Smith Shop Br of Little Cataba Cr; border: John Huggins sr on N side; includes a spring; entered Nov. 21, 1778; £3.14.

333. entry not to be "caried eney farther" by Ambrose Cobb Jan. 4, 1779; to be continued again Oct. 13, 1779; granted. Ambrose Cobb claims 150 ac in Tryon Co on S side of Cataba R; border: David Phillips and his own land; entered Nov. 26, 1778; £4.19.

334. granted. James Anderson claims 200 ac in Tryon Co on Sandy Run of First Broad R; below Logan's entry; includes William Hagerty's improvement; entered Nov. 26, 1778; £6.4.

Tryon County, NC Land Entries 1778-1779

335. granted. William Gilbert claims 200 ac in Tryon Co on head of Sheppards Cr and both sides of creek; border: his other entry on said creek; entered Nov. 29, 1778; £6.4.

336. granted. James Huey claims 100 ac in Tryon Co on both sides of Kain Cr; border: Jno Withrow and William Huddelstone; includes his own improvement; entered Nov. 29, 1778; £3.14.

page 73
337. granted. William Armstrong claims 150 ac in Tryon Cr on branch of Robinson Cr about 0.5 miles above Benjamin Biggerstaff; border: Lowry and John Kerkonel; includes his own improvement; entered Dec. 1, 1778; £4.19.

338. granted. Thomas Parker claims 200 ac in Tryon Co on Muddy fork of Buffeloe Cr; border: widow Caldwell and on both sides of water course; entered Dec. 1, 1778; £6.4.

339. granted. William Monday claims 150 ac in Tryon Co on Magness Cr; between Abel Beaty and Robert Wear's land he sold to John Skrimshire; entered Dec. 1, 1778; £4.19.

340. granted. John McIntire. Isam Blankenship claims 400 (written over 300) ac in Tryon Co on both sides of Gressey Br of First Broad R; includes William McKinney's improvement and a waggon road; entered Dec. 1, 1778; £8.14 + 2.10 = 11.4.

341. granted. John Walker claims 100 ac in Tryon Co on Kain Cr of Second Broad R; border: his own land; between David Huddlestone and Aaron Deviney; entered Dec. 1, 1778; £3.14.

page 74
342. granted. James Huddlestone claims 50 ac in Tryon Co on Kain Cr of Second Broad R; border: David Huddlestone and John Walker's entry #341; includes his own improvement; entered Dec. 1, 1778; £2.9.

343. granted. Moses Wright claims 100 ac in Tryon Co on both sides of Nob Cr of main Broad R; border and above: John Beard and below John McFadden; entered Dec. 1, 1778; £6.4 (sic).

344. granted to John McFadden; transmitted to James Latling & warrent granted to him. John McFadden (Moses Wright--lined out) claims 100 ac in Tryon Co on Nob Cr of main Broad R; border & above; John McClaim; includes fork of creek above McClain; entered Dec. 1, 1778; £3.14.

345. granted. David George claims 150 ac in Tryon Co on S side of Maple Cr;

Tryon County, NC Land Entries 1778-1779

border: Picerell, George Dukey, & his own land; entered Dec. 1, 1778; £4.19.

346. granted. Gideon Rucker claims 100 ac in Tryon Co on E side of Catheys Cr of Second Broad R; border: Thomas Morris on E side; entered Dec. 1, 1778; £3.14.

page 75
[insert] William Wilkins v Moses Scott--removed to Burke [Co].

347. granted. Jonathan Gullick (Joseph Henry--lined out) claims 100 ac in Tryon Co on waters of Mountain Cr; border: James Largent on NW and S "lines" and joining Winters; entered Dec. 1, 1788; £3.14.

348. granted to Jno Potts. John Potts (written over Thomas Morris) claims 100 ac in Tryon Co on Cedar Cr of main Broad R; border: Jonis Williams; includes mouth of Jumping Br; entered Dec. 1, 1778; £3.14.

349. granted. David Duckey claims 100 ac in Tryon Co on Cleghorne Cr; above Berry's survey; entered Dec. 1, 1778; £3.14.

350. discontinued & money paid back Aug. 4, 1779. Joseph Henry (Jonathan Gullick--lined out) claims 100 ac in Tryon Co on Horse Cr of N Pacolet R; near Alston and includes a shoal; entered Dec. 1, 1778; £3.14.

351. discontinued by Wright. Moses Wright claims 100 ac in Tryon Co on Mountain Cr "otherwise" Hamptons Mill Cr of main Broad R; above Hampton's upper survey on both sides of said creek; entered Dec. 1, 1778; £3.14.

page 76
352. granted. Allexandr McFadden claims 150 ac in Tryon Co on both sides of Mountain Cr of main Broad R; border & above: John McFadden desc and below Benjamin Hider; entered Dec. 4, 1778; £4.19.

353. granted. Thomas Rowland claims 100 ac in Tryon Co on Wheats Cr of Green R; border: Isaac Wilcocks and higher up the creek; includes James McFarland's improvement; entered Dec. 4, 1778; £3.14.

354. granted. Thomas Rowland claims 100 ac in Tryon Co on Brights Cr of Green R; includes Robert Mosely's improvement and a spring; entered Dec. 4, 1778; £3.14.

355. granted. Thomas Rowland claims 100 ac in Tryon Co on Balls Br of Catheys Cr of Second Broad R; border & above: Robert Melone's entry on said branch; entered Dec. 4, 1778; £3.14.

356. granted. Hugh Beaty claims 200 ac in Tryon Co on waters of Big Hicory

Tryon County, NC Land Entries 1778-1779

Cr; border: Wallace Beaty, John Sloan, & Nathaniel Kerr; entered Dec. 4, 1778; £6.4.

page 77
357. granted. John Thomason claims 100 ac in Tryon Co on Sizemores Cr of Second Broad R; above John Kyrkonel on said water course "on Jumping Br"; includes his own improvement; entered Dec. 4, 1778; £3.14.

358. granted. George Thomason claims 50 ac in Tryon Co on S side of main Broad R; border: Benjamin Townsend on W side; entered Dec. 4, 1778; £2.9.

359. granted. Michael Ozburn claims 50 ac on Floyds Cr of main Broad R; about 0.25 mile above William Thomason; includes his own improvement; entered Dec. 4, 1778; £2.9.

360. granted Apr. 1. John Camp claims 150 ac in Tryon Co on N side of Second Broad R; border & below: Richard Henderson and Mr Hill; includes his own improvement; entered Dec. 4, 1778; £4.19.

361. granted. James Camp claims 100 ac in Tryon Co on N side of Second Broad R; border & above: Richard Henderson; includes James Webb's improvement; entered Dec. 4, 1778; £3.14.

page 78
362. discontinued & money paid back Jul. 12, 1779. John Camp claims 50 ac in Tryon Co on main Broad R; border: John McKnit Allexander and George Saylors; above said Allexander's; entered Dec. 4, 1778; £2.9.

363. granted. David Liles claims 150 ac in Tryon Co on Ashworths Cr of Second Broad R about 4 miles "from mouth thereof"; entered Dec. 4, 1778; £4.19.

364. granted. Jonas Bedford claims 150 ac in Tryon Co on Ashworths Cr of Second Broad R about 0.25 mile below Liles' entry on said creek #363; entered Dec. 4, 178; £4.19.

365. granted. Jonas Bedford claims 100 ac in Tryon Co on Ashworths Cr of Second Broad R about 0.75 mile above Liles' entry #363; entry Dec. 4, 1778; £3.14.

366. granted. Jonas Bedford claims 100 ac in Tryon Co on Ashworths Cr of Second Broad R about 0.75 mile above his other entry #365; entered Dec. 4, 1778; £3.14.

page 79
367. granted. Raymond Bedford claims 640 ac in Tryon Co on Ashworths Cr of

Tryon County, NC Land Entries 1778-1779

Second Broad R about 1 mile above Jonas Bedford's entry on said creek #366; entered Dec. 4, 1778; £17.4.

368. granted. James Richesides (written over Jonas Bedford) claims 100 ac in Tryon Co Grogg Cr on Sandy Run of main Broad R about 1.5 mile below the path from high shoal to Capt. Kuyrkindal's; includes flat rock shoal in said creek; entered Dec, 4, 1778; £3.14.

369. granted. Jonas Bedford claims 150 ac in Tryon Co on Delseys Cr of main Broad R; about 1.25 miles from "mouth thereof"; includes a path from Barnet King's to "said" Delseys; entered Dec. 4, 1778; £4.19.

370. granted. John Camp (write over) claims 150 ac in Tryon Co on S side of Second Broad R; includes his own improvement; entered Dec. 4, 1778' £4.19.

371. granted. Thomas Warren claims 100 ac in Tryon Co on both sides of Ashworths Cr & at mouth of creek; includes his own improvement; entered Dec, 4, 1778; £3.14.

page 80
372. granted. William Webb claims 150 ac in Tryon Co on N side of Second Broad R; his own land on E side; entered Dec. 4, 1778; £4.19.

373. granted. John McClain claims 150 (200--lined out) ac in Tryon Co on Nob Cr of main Broad R; border: above John McFadden; includes John Stafford's improvement; entered Dec. 4, 1778; £4.19 (written over 6.4).

374. granted. James McFadden claims 150 ac in Tryon Co on branch of Maple Cr of main Broad R; border: William Lusk on N side; including the three forks of said branch; entered Dec. 4, 1778; £4.19.

375. granted. David Lewis claims 200 ac in Tryon Co on both sides of Cove Cr of main Broad R; includes his mill and improvement; entered Dec. 4, 1778; £6.4.

376. granted. David Lewis claims 200 ac in Tryon Co on both sides of Wheats Cr of main Broad R; border & below: Allexdr Mackey's entry; includes George Taylor's improvement; entered Dec. 4, 1778; £6.4.

page 81
377. granted. Isham Reavis claims 100 ac in Tryon Co on both sides of main Broad R; border: his own land he bought from John McFadden; border or near: Laughter; entered Dec. 4, 1778; £3.14.

378. granted to Wm Harmon by order of Reavis Oct. 30, 1779. Isham Revis claims 100 ac in Tryon Co on branch of Maple Cr; above James Dickey;

Tryon County, NC Land Entries 1778-1779

including the fork of the branch; entered Dec. 4, 1778; £3.14.

379. granted to John Jones by order of Reavis Oct. 30, 1779. Isham Reavis claims 100 ac in Tryon Co on both sides of Sinke hole Br waters of Mountain Cr of main Broad R; border: Dec. 4, 1778; £3.14.

380. granted. Allexander Mackey claims 100 (written over 200) ac in Tryon Co on N side of main Broad R; border: his own land and David Lewis; entered Dec. 4, 1778; £6.4.

381. granted. Jeremiah McDonald claims 200 ac in Tryon Co on S side of main Broad R; border: Twitty's South line and where said McDonald lives; entered Dec. 4, 1778; £6.4.

page 82
382. discontinued; money paid back Aug. 4, 1779. Joseph Henry claims 100 (written over 150) ac in Tryon Co on waters of Mountain Cr; border: William Eaves on W and S "side of said land"; entered Dec. 4, 1778; £4.19.

383. entry to be patented in Jas Holland's name Mar. 13, 1779; granted. Joseph Henry claims 200 ac in Tryon Co on waters of Mountain Cr of main Broad R; border: John Sorrel on N & W "sides of said land"; entered Dec. 4, 1778; £6.4.

384. granted. John Auston claims 150 ac in Tryon Co on Brights Cr of Green R; includes forks of said creek and a cabbin where Jas Step lived on N side of creek; entered Dec. 4, 1778; £4.19.

385. granted. John Sorrels claims 200 ac in Tryon Co on Mountain Cr of main Broad R; below Major Hampton on said creek; includes his own improvement; entered Dec. 4, 1778; £6.4.

386. granted. Samuel Hais claims 50 ac in Tryon Co on N side of Green R; border: Joseph McDaniel and his own land; entered Dec. 4, 1778; 1562.9.

page 83
387. granted. David Dickey claims 100 ac in Tryon Co on widow Cleghorne Cr of main Broad R; above widow Cleghorn on said creek; includes a shoal; entered Dec. 4, 1778; £3.14.
388. granted. William Gilbert claims 250 ac in Tryon Co on W side of Catheys Cr on branch thereof; nearly joining Bar on W side; includes Aaron Reily's improvement; extends "round the head of the branch"; entered Dec. 4, 1778; £7.9.

389. granted. William Gilbert claims 150 ac in Tryon Co on N fork of Walnut Cr; includes a "sapling flat" of land; entered Dec. 4, 1778; £4.19.

Tryon County, NC Land Entries 1778-1779

390. granted. James Logan calims 200 ac in Tryon Co on branch of Robinsons Cr; border: Aaron Biggerstaff higher up branch on N side; entered Dec. 4, 1778; £6.4.

391. granted. William Gilbert claims 200 ac in Tryon Co on the Shoal Br of Catheys Cr; border: his own land on N side; entered Dec. 4, 1778; £6.4.

page 84
392. granted. James Camp claims 200 ac in Tryon Co on both sides of Sizemores Cr of Second Broad R; below John Thomason's entry; entered Dec. 4, 1778; £6.4.

393. granted. Isham Reavis claims 200 ac in Tryon Co on Long Br of main Broad R; includes mouth of said branch and a skool house; border: his own land on N side; entered Dec. 5, 1778; £6.4.

394. granted. Abraham Muzick claims 100 ac in Tryon Co on waters of Wheats Cr; border: his own survey; includes Johnson's improvement; entered Dec. 5, 1778; £3.14.

395. granted. John Muzick claims 50 ac in Tryon Co on head waters of Skywicker Cr; known as Great Table of Tryon Mountion (county--lined out); includes his own improvement; entered Dec. 5, 1778; £2.9.

396. granted; discontinued Oct. 2, 1779. Isham Reavis claims 60 ac in Tryon Co on Hamptons Mill Cr; above Hampton's land; includes fork of the creek; entered Dec. 5, 1778; £2.14.

page 85
397. granted. George Davis claims 60 ac in Tryon Co on N side of Green R; border: Samuel French; includes Conaway's improvement; entered Dec. 5, 1778; £2.14.

398. granted. William Buntin claims 100 ac in Tryon Co on White Oak Cr of Green R; border: Jas Capshaw; includes a shoal and his own improvement; entered Dec. 5, 1778; £3.14.

399. granted. Thomas Justice claims 300 ac in Tryon Co on both sides of Green R; includes the Rock house and "downwards towards" Reily's entry; entered Dec. 5, 1778; £8.14.

400. granted May 29, 1779. Walter Butter claims 150 ac in Tryon Co on middle fork of White Oak Cr "otherwise" Jenkins fork; includes Charles Sayers improvement; entered Dec. 5, 1778; £4.19.

401. granted. Jonathan Oneal claims 100 ac in Tryon Co on a branch of White

Tryon County, NC Land Entries 1778-1779

Oak Cr; includes his own and Robert Edwards' improvements; entered Dec. 5, 1778; £3.14.

402. granted. Charles Sayers claims 50 ac in Tryon Co on a branch of White Oak Cr; border: Cleghorn and Jno Krykonel; includes his own improvement; entered Dec. 5, 1778; £2.9.

403. granted. John McFadden claims 200 ac in Tryon Co on Nob Cr of main Broad R; border: Jno McClaine and Beard; includes John Crawford's improvement; entered Dec. 5, 1778; £6.4.

404. caveated by Jas Step Dec. 9, 1778; discontinued by Aaron Reily Nov. 3, 1779. Aaron Reilly claims 100 ac in Tryon Co on both sides of Green R; below his own entry "and joining"; includes Jas Step's improvement; entered Dec. 5, 1778; £3.14.

405. granted. George Davis claims 100 ac in Tryon Co on N side of Green R; border: his own land on N side; entered Dec. 5, 1778; £3.14.

406. granted. Joseph McDaniel claims 100 ac in Tryon Co on N side of Green R on a branch that runs into Hutson's patented land; includes a path from Hutson's ford on Green R; entered Dec. 7, 1778; £3.14.

page 87
407. granted. Joseph McDaniel claims 100 ac in Tryon Co on branch of Green R (White Oak Cr--lined out); border: James Capshaw and Isaac Wilcocks; entered Dec. 7, 1778; £3.14.

408. granted May 23. Goerge Muzick claims 100 ac in Tryon Co on waters of Wheats Cr; border: Allexdr Mackey's "line below" and running up; entered Dec. 7, 1778; £3.14.

409. to be granted to Robert Allexdr Mar. 13, 1779; to be granted to Joseph Henry May 27, 1779; granted. Joseph Henry claims 200 ac in Tryon Co on N fork of White Oak Cr; includes Henry Adkins cabbins; border: begins below the forks of road near Alston's land "and up both sides"; entered Dec. 7, 1778; £6.4.

410. granted. Joseph Henry claims 100 (written over 200) ac in Tryon Co on Long Br of Jenkins fork of White Oak Cr; begins on N side of branch; entered Dec. 7, 1778; £3.14 (written over 6.4).

411. granted. Jervis Green claims 100 ac in Tryon Co on N fork of White Oak Cr; includes his own improvement; entered Dec. 8, 1778; £3.14.

page 88
412. granted May 27, 1779. Phillip Cokerhom claims 150 ac in Tryon Co on a

Tryon County, NC Land Entries 1778-1779

branch of White Oak Cr; border & above: Alston's "otherwise supposed to be" Sharp's land; includes where he now lives; entered Dec. 8, 1778; £4.19.

413. granted. Phillip Cokerhom claims 50 ac in Tryon Co on a branch of White Oak Cr; above his other entry; includes Mina Cokerhom's improvement; entered Dec. 8, 1778; £2.9.

414. granted. May (24?). Michael Hawkins claims 100 ac in Tryon Co on middle fork of White Oak Cr; includes his own improvement where he now lives; entered Dec. 8, 1778; £3.19.

415. granted Mar 26. John Cummins claims 150 ac in Tryon Co on S fork of White Oak Cr; near his own land; border: "a nob" on S side of creek; entered Dec. 8, 1778; £4.19.

416. granted. John Rotton claims 100 ac in Tryon Co on both sides of Green R above Alstons Cr; includes his own improvement; entered Dec. 8, 1778; £3.14.

page 89
417. granted. Allen Hinson claims 50 ac in Tryon Co on Bullions Cr of Green R about a mile from "mouth thereof"; includes his own improvement; entered Dec. 8, 1778; £2.9.

418. granted. Mar. 26. Jonathan Gullick claims 50 ac in Tryon Co on Cummins Cr of White Oak Cr; border & above: Cummins' land on said creek; entered Dec. 8, 1778; £2.9.

419. entered by Aaron Reily Dec. 5, 1778; granted to James Step Nov. 3, 1779. James Step claims 50 ac in Tryon Co on N side of Green R (White Oak--lined out); includes his own improvement; entered Dec. 9, 1778; £2.9.

420. granted to Jas Logan. Thomas Sprigs claims 150 ac in Tryon Co on main fork of White Oak Cr; nearly joining Essex Capshaw on E side; includes "both" the improvement below; entered Dec. 9, 1778; £4.19.

421. granted in hane (or Harce) name; discontinued. Jas Logan and George Davis claims 100 ac in Tryon Co on S fork of Brights Cr of Green R; border: Auston's entry; includes Dollom's improvement; entered Dec. 9, 1778; £3.14.

page 90
422. granted. Joseph McDaniel claims 300 ac in Tryon Co on both sides of Green R; border & above: Hutson; includes his own improvement; entered Dec. 9, 1778; £8.14.

423. granted. Peter Queen claims 500 ac in Tryon Co on W side of Little Broad R; border: Armstrong on N side; includes his two improvements and Reedy Br

Tryon County, NC Land Entries 1778-1779

boundary on the river; entered Dec. 12, 1778; £13.14.

424. granted Apr. 14. Jonathan Gullick claims 100 ac in Tryon Co on Little Cr on S side of N Pacolet R; about 1.5 mile from mouth of said creek; entered Dec. 12, 1778; £3.14.

425. granted. James Logan claims 100 ac in Tryon Co on middle fork of Skiewicker Cr of N Pacolet R; includes (ink blob) white oak land above forks thereof; entered Dec. 12, 1778; £3.14.

426. granted in Gullick's name. Jonathan Gullick [and?] James Logan claims 100 ac in Tryon Co on Varons Cr of N Pacolet R; near 2 miles from mouth thereof; includes upper part of a shoal and that flat known as Sep (or Gep) Jones camp; entered Dec. 12, 1778; £3.14.

page 91
427. granted in Logan's name. Jonathan Gullick and Jas Logan claims 50 (write over) ac in Tryon Co on Vawns Cr; border: Sprigg's entry; includes Vawn's old cabbin and lower shoal of said creek; entered Dec. 12, 1778; £2.9 (write over).

428. granted. James Logan claims 50 (100--lined out) ac in Tryon Co on N Pacolet R; above Thomas Sprigg's entry on Little Kane Cr; entered Dec. 12, 1778; £2.9 (3.14--lined out).

429. granted. James Logan claims 100 ac in Tryon Co on N Pacolet R; above his other entry on said river; includes Hooper's camps; entered Dec. 12, 1778; £3.14.

430. granted to James Webb (write over) by bargin of Logan Oct. 30, 1779. James Logan claims 200 ac in Tryon Co on Ashworths Cr of Second Broad R; near a mile from mouth on both sides of creek; includes John Turner's improvement; entered Dec. 12, 1778; £6.4.

431. granted. James Logan claims 100 ac in Tryon Co on Little Cataba Cr; border: Adam Carruth and his own land; entered Dec. 12, 1778; £3.14.

page 92
432. granted. William Waddle claims 150 ac in Tryon Co on Muddy fork of Buffeloe Cr; border & above: Hugh Erwin on both sides of creek and on N side of Erwin; entered Dec. 23, 1778; £4.19.

433. granted to James Hicks. James Hicks (write over) claims 200 (write over) ac in Tryon Co on creek that Daniel Blackwell lives on; about 0.5 mile above Blackwell; on both sides of raod from Richardson's mill to the high shoal on Little Broad R; entered Dec. 24, 1778; £6.4 (write over).

Tryon County, NC Land Entries 1778-1779

434. granted to James Kitchisides. James Kitchisides (write over) claims 200 (written over 150) ac in Tryon Co on both sides of Groggs Cr of Second Broad R; includes where Abraham Kuyrkindall now holds his muster; entered Dec. 24, 1778; £8.14 (sic).

435. granted. Phelimon Hawkins claims 150 ac in Tryon Co on N side of main Broad R; border: above William Hawkins' land "he" bought from Jonas Bedford and below Peter Dills "between those surveys"; entered Dec. 24, 1778; £4.19.

436. granted. Frederwick Hambright claims 200 ac in Tryon Co on both sides of Wards Cr of First Broad R; border: William Goings and Thomas Black; includes a shoal on said creek; entered Dec. 25, 1778; £6.4.

page 93
437. granted. Daniel Wiatt sr claims 200 ac in Tryon Co on waters of Little Long Cr; border: Peter Carpenter, James Wiatt, & Ezekiel Hezlet; includes George Martin's improvement; entered Dec. 26, 1778; £6.4.

438. entry discontinued by Jas Wiatt Dec. 29, 1778. James Wiatt claims 100 ac in Tryon Co on N side of Little Long Cr; border: Peter Carpenter and land claimed by Thomas Hawkins, & Edward Jenkins' entry; includes his own improvement; entered Dec. 26, 1778; £3.14.
439. granted. Aaron Reily claims 300 ac in Tryon Co on S side of Muddy fork of Buffeloe Cr; includes Edward Hampton's improvement on both sides of waggon road from Tryon Court house to Able Beaty's and "running over towards the Pitsimon branches"; entered Dec. 26, 1778; £8.14.

440. granted. John Dilbeck claims 150 ac in Tryon Co on N side of main Broad R; border: John Webb; includes his own improvement; entered Dec. 26, 1778; £4.19.

441. granted. Joseph Logan claims 200 ac in Tryon Co on both sides of First Broad R; border: Beaty's lower line; includes his own improvement; entered Dec. 26, 1778; £4.19.

page 94
442. granted. Joseph Gregory claims 100 ac in Tryon Co on E side of First Broad R; border: Andrew Hezlep; includes his own improvement; entered Dec. 26, 1778; £3.14.

443. granted Jun. 2. Richard Skruggs claims 150 ac in Tryon Co on N side of main Broad R; in forks between main Broad and Second Broad R; includes his own improvement where he now lives; entered Dec. 26, 1778; £4.19.

444. granted. Samuel White claims 200 ac in Tryon Co on both sides of Little Long Cr; border: Michael Hoyl, George Beasour (or Beajour), & Peter Laboon;

Tryon County, NC Land Entries 1778-1779

includes Allexander Laboon's improvement; entered Dec. 26, 1778; £6.4.

445. granted. David Miller claims 100 ac in Tryon Co on Green Br of Mountain Cr waters of main Broad R; includes Richard Daugherty's improvement; entered Dec. 27, 1778; £3.14.

446. granted Jun. 2. David Miller claims 50 ac in Tryon Co on main Broad R; on Wi side of James Miller; includes John Cowsar's improvement; entered Dec. 27, 1778; £2.9.

page 95
447. granted. James Webb claims 250 ac in Tryon Co on a large branch on N side of Second Broad R; branch runs through William Webb's land; includes Jas Webb jr's improvement on both sides of creek; entered Dec. 27, 1778; £7.9.

448. granted. David Liles claims 150 ac in Tryon Co on N side of Second Broad R; border: Swan; includes Mosely Owens' improvement; entered Dec. 27, 1778; £4.19.

449. granted. William Collins claims 100 ac in Tryon Co on Rockey Br of Second Broad R; on E side of Thos Warren's entry nearly joining same; includes his own improvement; entered Dec. 27, 1778; £3.14.

450. granted. Lott Warren claims 100 ac in Tryon Co; "nearly joining" Able Hill's land on S side; about 300 yds from said Hill's fence; entered Dec. 27, 1778; £3.14.

451. granted. Edmund Wyatt claims 200 ac in Tryon Co on Long Br of Little Long Cr; border: Foster Sims and Ezekiel Hezlet; includes his own improvement; entered Dec. 29, 1778; £6.4.

page 96
452. granted. James Wyat claims 200 ac in Tryon Co on both sides of Little Long Cr; border: Peter Carpenter, George Palmer, Edward Jenkins, land claimed by Thos Hawkins, & Horton; includes his own improvement; entered Dec. 29, 1778; £6.14 (sic).

453. caveated by Wm Varnor Mar. 26, 1779. George Palmer claims 100 ac in Tryon Co on Meadow Br of Little Long Cr; border: his own land on N side; entered Dec. 29, 1778; £3.14.

454. granted. John McClain sr claims 50 ac in Tryon Co on both sides of Nob (or Hob) Cr of main Broad R; includes a shoal; border: Land Thomas Herod sold to John Beard; entered Dec. 31, 1778; £2.9.

455. discontinued by Joseph Henry Jul. 12, 1779. Joseph Henry claims 150 ac in

Tryon County, NC Land Entries 1778-1779

Tryon Co on both sides of Sandy Run of Broad R; includes Abednego Green's improvement where "he" now lives; entered Dec. 31, 1778; £4.19.

456. granted; discontinued. John McClain jr claims 64 (100--lined out) ac in Tryon Co on both sides of main Broad R; border: John McClain sr and Twitty; entered Dec. 31, 1778; £2.10 (write over).

page 97

457. granted. John Dillinger claims 200 ac in Tryon Co on Little Br of Indian Cr on S fork of Cataba R; border: John Allexander and his own land "on N side"; entered Jan. 1, 1779; £6.4.

458. granted. John Dillinger claims 200 ac in Tryon Co on waters of Indian Cr of S fork of Cataba R; border: land Peter Carpenter brought from Aaron More on N side; entered Jan. 1, 1779; £6.4.

459. 100 ac of this entry caveated by Geo Palmer Mar. 1779. William Vernor claims 200 ac in Tryon Co on waters of Little Long Cr; border: Michael Hoyl, George Palmer, & Low; includes Robert Mitchell's improvement; entered Jan. 1, 1779; £6.4.

460. granted Jun. 2. John Hoyl claims 50 ac in Tryon Co on both sides of Little Long Cr; above his own land; entered Jan. 2, 1779; £2.9.

461. granted to Isaac West. John Cobb claims 300 ac in Tryon Co on both sides of Dutchmans Cr of S fork of Cataba R; border: Rutledge, West, Jas Miligan, & land Polk bought from Wm More; entered Jan. 4, 1779; £8.14.

page 98

462. granted. James Armstrong claims 250 ac in Tryon Co on Shoal Br of Little Shoal Cr of S fork of Cataba R; border: Wm Graham, Ramsey, & Wm Armstrong jr's entry; includes his own improvement; entered Jan. 8, 1779; £7.9.

463. granted. John Ensly claims 250 ac in Tryon Co on head of Williams Br and near branch of Buffeloe Cr; border: Williams on E side; entered Jan. 8, 1779; £7.9.

464. granted. John Ensly claims 200 ac in Tryon Co on waters of Bufeloe Cr; on road from Carson's to Hardin's "where Murphey's road comes into waggon road"; entered Jan. 8, 1779; £6.4.

465. granted Jul. 16, 1779. John Ensley claims 150 ac in Tryon Co on waters of Long Br of Buffeloe Cr; between John Allexandr and James Carson; entered Jan. 8, 1779; £4.19.

466. discontinued by Elisha Herd Castle Jan. 13, 1779. Elisha Herd Castle claims 200 ac in Tryon Co on Muddy fork of Buffeloe Cr; about 1 mile above

Tryon County, NC Land Entries 1778-1779

Adam Neil; includes upper fork of the creek; entered Jan. 8, 1779; £6.4.

466A. granted. Zakariah Salurs claims 300 ac in Tryon Co on waters of Hicory Cr; includes Charles Borinss improvement; entered Jan. 8, 1779; £8.14.

page 99
467. granted. William Porter claims 100 ac in Tryon Co on S side of Catheys Cr; border: Cook and his own land; includes William Daves improvement; entered Jan. 8, 1779; £3.14.

468. granted. David Porter claims 100 in Tryon Co on branch of Camp Cr of Second Broad R; border: his own land on W side; entered Jan. 8, 1779; £3.14.

469. granted to John McKinney by order from Terry Dec. 6, 1779. William Tery claims 100 ac in Tryon Co on S fork of White Oak Cr; border & above: George Potts; includes a shoal; entered Jan. 8, 1779l; £3.14.

470. granted. William Baker claims 50 ac in Tryon Co on Cherokee Br of Second Broad R; border: Robert Clinton and his own land; includes Richard Fleming's improvement; entered Jan. 8, 1779; £3.14.

471. granted. John Matox claims 200 ac in Tryon Co on McMurreys Br of Cataba R; border: Leper and Jas Beaty "otherwise" Robert Gray; entered Jan. 11, 1779; £3.14.

page 100
472. granted. John Gullick jr claims 150 ac in Tryon Co on a branch of White Oak Cr; border: William Capshaw; includes Edward Holder's improvement where "he" now lives; entered Jan. 11, 1779; £4.19.

473. granted. William More claims 150 ac in Tryon Co on N side of branch of Green R; includes Joseph Burgess' improvement; where "he" now lives; entered Jan. 11, 1779; £4.19.

474. granted. William Berry claims 150 ac in Tryon Co on middle fork of White Oak Cr; border: Sharp; includes Jenkins' improvement; entered Jan. 11, 1779; £4.19.

475. granted. Benjamin Hydar claims 200 ac in Tryon Co on waters of Mountain Cr; border: McClean and his own land; entered Jan. 11, 1779; £6.4.

476. granted Jul. 16, 1779. John Potts claims 100 ac in Tryon Co on Morris Cr of Cove Cr; includes John McKealy's improvement; border: his own land; entered Jan. 11, 1779; £3.14.

page 101

Tryon County, NC Land Entries 1778-1779

477. granted May 1, 1779. William Grant claims 150 ac in Tryon Co on Grants Cr of Cove Cr; "at a place known by McNealy's timber tree"; entered Jan. 11, 1779; £4.19.

478. granted to Thomas Jostice. James McFarlen claims 100 ac in Tryon Co on both sides of Green R; above Spencer's entry; entered Jan. 11, 1779; £3.14.

479. granted. Joseph Williams claims 100 ac in Tryon Co on both sides of middle fork of White Oak Cr; border: Soloman White "below" and Quinn "above"; includes his own improvement; entered Jan. 11, 1779; £3.14.

480. granted to Jas Logan. Jeremiah Smith claims 150 ac in Tryon Co on S side of Horse Cr of main Broad R; includes Richard Hicks' improvement; entered Jan. 11, 1779; £4.19.

481. granted; discontinued. Jonas Bedford claims 100 ac in Tryon Co on S side of main Broad R above Island ford; border: the river; includes where Shadrach Elkins made an improvement; "above his head rights"; entered Jan. 11, 1779; £6.0 (sic).

page 102
482. granted; discontinued. Jeremiah Smith claims 150 ac in Tryon Co on S side of main Broad R; below ford where Gilbert's road crosses "that leads to Charles Town"; includes Andrew Poors improvement; entered Jan. 11, 1779; £4.19.

483. granted. Jas Logan. John Hedley (write over) claims 150 ac in Tryon Co on a branch of Sandy Run; includes Forney Green Norman's improvement; entered Jan. 11, 1779; £4.19.

484. granted; discontinued. Jonas Bedford claims 50 ac in Tryon Co on Floyds Cr of main Broad R; includes widow Wheat's improvement; "above" his head rights; entered Jan. 11, 1779; £3.14.

485. granted Jul. 16 to Gray Briggs. Samuel Richardson claims 200 ac in Tryon Co on Hughes Cr of N Pacolet R; border: Christopher Plunket; includes his own improvement; entered Jan. 11, 1779; £6.4.

486. granted. Elisha Hard Castle claims 50 ac in Tryon Co on Crowders Cr; above Wm Morison's land on same branch; includes Isaac Kimbol's improvement; entered Jan. 14, 1779; £2.9.

page 103
487. granted. William Hall claims 100 ac in Tryon Co on both sides of Richland Cr of Green R; border: William Mills jr on N side; entered Jan. 15, 1779; £3.14.

488. granted to Isham Reves by order of Kersey Oct. 30, 1779. Randolf Kersey claims 100 ac in Tryon Co on Godfreys Br of main Broad R; border: Walker on

Tryon County, NC Land Entries 1778-1779

N side; includes where a cabbin was built and mouth of said branch; entered Jan. 15, 1779; £3.14.

489. granted; discontinued Oct. 2, 1779. William Hall claims 100 ac in Tryon Co on branch of Green R about 1 mile from Ambrose Mills; border: land claimed by Ambrose Mills where Wm Mills sr now lives; entered Jan. 15, 1779; £3.14.

490. granted. Randolph Kersey claims 100 ac in Tryon Co on S fork of Mountain Cr of main Broad R; includes upper ford of said creek where Cove road crosses; entered Jan. 15, 1779; £3.14.

491. granted. Randolph Kersey claims 50 ac in Tryon Co on both sides of Green R; border: Wm Mills; includes John Stuart's improvement; entered Jan. 15, 1779; £2.9.

page 104
492. granted. Adlai Ozburn claims 150 ac in Tryon Co on both sides of N Pacolet R; known as Little Kane Break; above Jas Logan's entry on said river; entered Jan. 15, 1779; £4.19.

493. granted. Allexander McIntire claims 200 ac in Tryon Co on E side of main Broad R on Johnsons Br; above Dihes ford on said river; includes his own improvement; entered Jan. 15, 1779; £6.4.

494. granted. William Hall claims 50 ac in Tryon Co on Metcalfs Br of N side of Green R; includes old Storey's improvement where Joseph Barges lives; entered Jan. 15, 1779; £2.9.

495. granted. Jul. 16, 1779. Jonathan Harding claims 250 ac in Tryon Co on waters of Little Hicory Cr; border: his own land; includes Allexander McIntire's camp; entered Jan. 20, 1779; £4.19.

496. granted. James Saterfield claims 100 ac in Tryon Co on Beaverdam Cr of Little Broad R; above James Logan's land; includes his own improvement; entered Jan. 20, 1779; £3.14.

page 105
497. granted. James Satterfield claims 200 ac in Tryon Co on head of Yanceys Br of Little Broad R; includes his own improvement; entered Jan. 20, 1779; £6.4.

498. granted. Christian Hogans claims 90 ac on N sides of Green R on Edward Hogans spring branch; border: said Hogan on N side; entered Jan. 20, 1779; £3.9.

Tryon County, NC Land Entries 1778-1779

499. granted. John Turner claims 100 ac in Tryon Co on Ashworths Cr on S side of main Broad R; includes his own improvement; entered Jan. 20, 1779; £3.14.

500. granted. Samuel Turner claims 100 ac in Tryon Co on E side of Beaver Cr on N side of main Broad R; includes his own improvement; entered Jan. 20, 1779; £3.14.

501. granted. Nicholas Fisher claims 100 ac in Tryon Co on Beaverdam Cr of First Broad R; border: Turner's and Saterfield;s entrys and John Richerds(?); includes his own improvement; entered Jan. 20, 1779; £3.14.

page 106
502. granted. John Fisher claims 100 ac in Tryon Co on Beaverdam Cr of First Broad R; includes his own improvement; border: John Richmond; entered Jan. 20, 1779; £3.14.

503. granted. James Ellis claims 250 ac in Tryon Co on S side of main Broad R; border: South Carolina state line and his own land; includes a small improvement; entered Jan. 20, 1779; £4.19.

504. granted. Benjamin Harding claims 100 ac in Tryon Co on Little Hicory Cr of First Broad R; border: Morris Roberts; includes his own improvement; entered Jan. 20, 1779; £3.14.

505. [not in book; skip in numbers.]

506. granted. William Byers claim 200 ac in Tryon Co on Towsends Br of main Broad R; border: Towsend; includes his own improvement; entered Jan. 20, 1779; £6.4.

507. granted Nov. 2, 1779. Thomas Camp claims 200 ac on S side of main Broad R "fornenst" [border?] Hawkins Shoal on said river; includes his own improvement; entered Jan. 20, 1779; £6.4.

page 107
508. granted. Thomas Camp claims 100 (written over 50) ac in Tryon Co on S side of main Broad R; above Pools Br; includes John Wilson's improvement; entered Jan. 20, 1779; £3.14 (written over 2.2).

509. granted. Thomas Camp claims 50 ac in Tryon Co on N side of main Broad R; includes Camp's landing and improvement; entered Jan. 20, 1779; £2.9.

510. granted. Josua Burnet (or Burnes) claims 100 ac in Tryon Co on waters of Big Hicory Cr of First Broad R; border: John Sloan; includes his own improvement; entered Jan. 20, 1779; £3.14.

Tryon County, NC Land Entries 1778-1779

511. granted. Nathan Camp claims 200 ac in Tryon Co on Sandy Run of main Broad R; border: Abraham Kuyrkindal; includes where said Camp lives; entered Jan. 20, 179; £6.4.

512. granted. Benjamin Camp claims 100 ac in Tryon Co on Sandy Run of main Broad R; above William Johnson's "patoned" land; includes Benjamin Camp's improvement; entered Jan. 20, 1779; £3.14.

page 108
513. granted. Nathan Camp claims 100 ac in Tryon Co; border: "line of South state"; includes his own improvement and head of Glady Meadow Br on Serrats Cr; entered Jan. 20, 1779; £3.14.

514. granted. William Humphreys claims 100 ac in Tryon Co on Turners Br of Serrats Cr of main Broad R; includes his own improvement; entered Jan. 20, 1779; £3.14.

515. discontinued by John Wire Jul. 20, 1779. John Wire claims 200 ac in Tryon Co on Solomans Cr of Buffeloe Cr; border: John Robinson and Wm Morris' entry; includes Nicholas Walton's improvement; entered Jan. 20, 1779; £6.4.

516. granted. John Anderson claims 100 ac in Tryon Co on S side of main Broad R; border: Mathew Guthery and Thomas Camp; includes his own improvement; entered Jan. 20, 1779; £3.14.

517. granted. Benjamin Williams claims 200 ac in Tryon Co on Yanceys Br of First Broad R; about 1.5 miles above Allexdr Davidson; includes improvements he bought from Moses Bridges; entered Jan. 20, 1779; £6.4.

page 109
518. granted. George Woolf claims 200 ac in Tryon Co on Howards Cr of N Pacolet R; above Townsend [and] Robinson on said creek; includes his own improvement; entered Jan. 20, 1779; £6.4.

519. granted to Edmond Kanady by order of Shipman. Joseph Shipman claims 200 ac in Tryon Co on both sides of Sandy Run of main Broad R; border: Thomas Rannolds and Timothey Riggs; includes his three improvements; entered Jan. 20, 1779; £6.4.

520. granted. Robert Webb claims 50 ac in Tryon Co on S side of Second Broad R; about 0.75 mile above Jeremiah Webb; includes Burrel Sims' improvement; entered Jan. 20, 1779; £2.9.

521. granted. William Baker claims 100 ac in Tryon Co on left hand fork of Webbs Cr of Second Broad R; above and near: Kuyrkindal; includes Daniel Gage's improvement; entered Jan. 20, 1779; £3.14.

Tryon County, NC Land Entries 1778-1779

522. granted. James Miller sr claims 200 ac in Tryon Co on both sides of main Broad R; border: John McClure; higher up river than McClure; includes his own improvement; entered Jan. 20, 1779; £3.14.

page 110
523. granted Logan's name. Jas Logan and James Miller sr claim 150 (written over 100) ac in Tryon Co on branch of Cleghorns Cr of main Broad R; border: Berry and his own land on W side; entered Jan. 20, 1779; £4.19 (written over 3.14).

524. granted. Isaac Rice claims 100 ac in Tryon Co on Shoal Cr of Little Broad R; border: Jas Crow and Jonathan Harding; includes his own improvement; entered Jan. 20, 1779; £3.14.

525. [not in book; skip in numbers.]

526. granted. Joseph Vawn claims 150 ac in Tryon Co on Bear Cr of N Pacolet R; about 1 mile from line of South sate; includes his own improvement; entered Jan. 20, 1779; £4.19.

527. granted to George Ledbetter Oct. 17, 1783 (sic). James Morris claims 150 ac in Tryon Co on Second Cr of Cove Cr; includes his own improvement; border: steep gulley on N side of said creek; entered Jan. 20, 1779; £4.19.

528. granted. Moses Rice claims 150 ac in Tryon Co on Shoal Cr of Little Broad R; border: Isaac Rice's entry; includes his own improvement; entered Jan. 20, 1779; £4.19.

page 111
529. granted. John Dever claims 100 ac in Tryon Co on Long Br of Buffeloe Cr; border: Joseph Glading; includes his own improvement; entered Jan. 20, 1779; £3.14.

530. granted. William Smith claims 200 ac in Tryon Co on waters of Big Hicory Cr; border: Beaty and John Waterson; includes his own improvement; entered Jan. 20, 1779; £6.4.

531. granted. David Lewis claims 200 ac in Tryon Co on Broad R; includes David Cocks and "his" father's improvements on both sides of river; entered Jan. 20, 1779; £6.4.

532. granted. George Fleming claims 200 ac in Tryon Co on both sides of Cleghorns Br above the shoals; entered Jan. 20, 1779; £6.4.

533. granted. John Flack claims 80 ac in Tryon Co on both sides of Catheys Cr;

Tryon County, NC Land Entries 1778-1779

border: his own land; entered Jan. 20, 1779; £3.4 (? ink blob).

page 112
534. granted. John Flack claims 200 ac in Tryon Co "in the Cove"; border: tree marked "IF" and John Potts on Cove Cr; entered Jan. 20, 1779; £6.4.

535. granted. John Black claims 100 ac in Tryon Co "in the Cove"; border: branch of Cove Cr and tree marked "C" or "B"; a little below Phillip Goodbread's old improvement; entered Jan. 20, 1779; £3.14.

536. granted to Mathew Paterson Apr. 1783. William McGahey claims 100 ac in Tryon Co on Puzzel Cr of Second Broad R; border: John Kuyrkonel and Langham; includes his own improvement; entered Jan. 20, 1779; £3.14.

537. granted. David Harding claims 100 ac in Tryon Co on head of Calf pen Br of Buffeloe Cr; border: Jonathan Harding's entry; entered Jan. 20, 1779; £3.14.

538. granted. Allexander Coulter claims 100 ac in Tryon Co on Bullions Cr of Green R; about 1 mile above Allon Hinson; includes an old improvement; entered Jan. 20, 1779; £3.14.

page 113
539. discontinued by Jas Polly & money paid back Jul. 22, 1779. James Polly claims 200 ac in Tryon Co on Locust Ridge Br of Muddy fork of Buffeloe Cr; border: Joseph Dixon and near Christian Money; entered Jan. 20, 1779; £6.4.

540. granted. James Polly claims 200 ac in Tryon Co on Muddy fork of Buffeloe Cr; border: his own land and Abraham Barnet; entered Jan. 21, 1779; £6.4.

541. discontinued; money paid back Jul. 12, 1779. Stephen Willis claims 400 ac in Tryon Co on S fork of Mountain Cr of main Broad R; above John Sorrel and near a shoal on both sides of side creek; entered Jan. 21, 1779; £11.4.

542. granted. Allexander Mackey claims 200 ac in Tryon Co on N fork of White Oak Cr of Green R; border: Queen and on both sides of creek; includes John Owen's improvement; entered Jan. 21, 1779; £6.4.

543. granted. Samuel White claims 300 ac in Tryon Co on NW side of Little Long Cr; border: Peter Labooon on W side; entered Jan. 21, 1779; £8.4.

page 114
544. granted. John Allexander claims 100 ac in Tryon Co in fork between Indian Cr and S fork of Cataba R; border: his own land on N side; includes his own improvement "on his open line"; entered Jan. 21, 1779; £3.14.

545. granted. John Allexandr claims 50 ac in Tryon Co on Indian Cr on S fork of

Tryon County, NC Land Entries 1778-1779

Cataba R; border: his own land on S side; includes his own improvement; entered Jan. 21, 1779; £2.9.

546. granted. Joel Shilton claims 150 ac in Tryon Co on Corn field fork of Beaverdam Cr of Little Broad R; about 1.5 mile above Samuel Blackburn; includes his own improvement; entred Jan. 21, 1779; £4.19.

547. granted. Joel Shilton claims 100 ac in Tryon Co on Corn field fork of Beaverdam Cr of Little Broad R; about 1.5 mile above Saml Blackburn and joins his other entry on N side; includes his own improvement; entered Jan. 21, 1779; £3.14.

548. entry discontinued by Coleclough & money paid back. Benjamin Coleclough claims 50 ac in Tryon Co on Wolf Pit Br on S side of main Broad R; border: Beard; entered Jan. 21, 1779; £2.9.

page 155

549. granted. Andrew Hampton claims 200 ac in Tryon Co; border: his own land on both forks of Mountain Cr; entered Jan. 21, 1779; £6.4.

550. discontinued Oct. 2, 1779. Andrew Hampton claims 60 ac in Tryon Co; includes Shadrach Nettles' improvement at head of Sheppards Cr; entered Jan. 21, 1779; £2.14.

551. granted. Martha Douglas claims 100 ac in Tryon Co on fork of Boreings Cr; border: Hugh Queen; includes her own improvement; entered Jan. 21, 1779; £3.14.

552. granted. William Logan claims 500 ac in Tryon Co on Boreings Cr of main Broad R; border: Hugh Queen on NE side; includes his own improvement and Wm Parker's; entered Jan. 21, 1779; £3.14.

553. granted. Joseph Bradley claims 100 ac in Tryon Co on Williams Cr of First Broad R; border: Joseph Spencer; includes his own improvement; entered Jan. 21, 1779; £3.14.

page 116

554. granted. Joseph Grayson claims 50 ac in Tryon Co on both sides of Long Br of N fork of Broad R; border: Thomas Whitesides and Burke's line; includes a small improvement; entered Jan. 21, 1779; £2.9.

555. granted. Allexander Baldridge claims 20 ac in Tryon Co on Cataba R; "being an island"; border: John Cowen and Allexander Wills; entered Jan. 21, 1779; £1.14.

556. granted. John Blankinship claims 200 ac in Tryon Co on head of Harris Cr of First Broad R; includes his own improvement; entered Jan. 21, 1779; £6.4.

Tryon County, NC Land Entries 1778-1779

557. granted. Michael McElwrath claims 50 ac in Tryon Co on Cedar Cr of Cove Cr; border: his own land on N side; includes the little kane bread; entered Jan. 21, 1779; £2.9.

558. granted. Michael McElwrath claims 50 ac in Tryon Co on main Cove Cr; border: his own land on NE side; entered Jan. 21, 1779; £2.9.

page 117
559. granted to Thomas Whitesides. Samuel Moor calims 50 ac in Tryon Co on Hintons Cr of First Broad R; border: Nicolas Leper on W side; includes his owm improvement; entered Jan. 21, 1779; £2.9.

560. granted to Thomas Whitesides. Samuel More claims 50 ac in Tryon Co on Hintons Cr of First Broad R; includes improvement where Wm Harris lived "that was made by Wm Armstrong"; entered Jan. 21, 1779; £2.9.

561. granted. Thomas Potter claims 100 ac in Tryon Co on both sides of Green R; above his "former land" on said river; includes part of his improvement; entered Jan. 21, 1779; £3.14.

562. discontinued by David Miller Oct. 4, 1779. David Miller claims 100 ac in Tryon Co on Greens Cr of Mountain Cr; border: Green and Bedford; entered Jan. 21, 1779; £3.14.

563. granted. Benjamin Lindsey claims 300 ac in Tryon Co near heads of Kings Cr; border: Thos Dixon and on both sides of waggon road to Charles Town and near gap in Kings Mountain; entered Jan. 21, 1779; £8.14.

page 118
564. granted in Miller's name. Jas Logan and Jas Miller, sherif, claim 50 ac in Tryon Co on Maple Cr of Mountain Cr; border: "his" lower place and James Dickey; entered Jan. 22, 1779; £2.9.

565. granted. Thomas Donaldson claims 100 ac in Tryon Co on middle fork of Catheys Cr of Second Broad R; "close under the mountain"; border: Jas Black on E side; includes his own improvement; entered Jan. 22, 1779; £3.14.

566. granted. Robert Wire claims 200 ac in Tryon Co on both sides of Long Br of Buffeloe Cr; border: Wm Magness and George Wizenhant; entered Jan. 22, 1779; £6.4.

567. granted. David Miller claims 100 ac in Tryon Co on both sides of Bills Cr at Cove ford at foot of Bills Mountain; includes a shoal and Harrison's improvement; entered Jan. 22, 1779; £3.14.

568. granted. Thomas White claims 200 ac in Tryon Co at head of Uleys Br of Long Cr; border: Jas White; entered Jan. 22, 1779; £6.4.

Tryon County, NC Land Entries 1778-1779

page 119
569. granted to Samuel Rankin. James Rutledge claims 150 ac in Tryon Co on waters of Dutchmans Cr of Cataba R; nearly joining: Adam Cloninger and his own land; entered Jan. 22, 1779; £4.19.

570. to be granted to Joseph Camp through warrent; granted. (William Yancey--lined out) claims 250 (300--lined out) ac in Tryon Co on W side of main Broad R opposite mouth of First Broad R; includes Joseph Camp's improvement; entered Jan. 22, 1779; £7.9 (8.14--lined out).

571. granted. James Holland claims 200 ac in Tryon Co on Long Br of Buffeloe Cr; includes a meadow above Swaffort's land; on E side of Robert Wair's claims "which lies on Hicory Br"; entered Jan. 22, 1779; £6.4.

572. granted. William Clark Johnson claims 300 ac in Tryon Co on Hendersons Cr of Second Broad R; about a mile above John Pain's land; includes Gash Lee's improvement; entered Jan. 22, 1779; £8.14.

573. granted. Nicolas Clark claims 200 ac in Tryon Co on head of Shoal Cr on Second Broad R; entered Jan. 22, 1779; £6.4.

page 120
574. granted. Joseph Clark claims 200 ac in Tryon Co on Hog Pen Br of Second Broad R; includes Rock Spring and where said Clark cut house logs; entered Jan. 22, 1779; £6.4.

575. granted. William Groves claims 200 ac in Tryon Co on Flat Rock Br of Crowders Cr; border: Ambrose Foster, John McFarland, & Hugh Torrance; includes his own improvements; entered Jan. 22, 1779; £6.4.

576. discontinued Jun. 5, 1779. William Armstrong jr claims 200 ac in Tryon Co on Kittles Cr of S fork of Cataba R; border: Nicholas Friday, Wm Armstrong sr or James Armstrong jr's entry, & Ramsey; entered Jan. 22, 1779; £6.4.

577. granted. Saml Hendricks claims 50 ac in Tryon Co on Bills Cr of Cove Cr; below William Nettles; includes his own improvement; entered Jan. 22, 1779; £2.9.

578. granted. Stephen Shilton claims 200 ac in Tryon Co on Bills Cr of Cove Cr; above William Nettles; includes his own improvement; entered Jan. 22, 1779; £6.4.

page 121
579. granted. Isaac Harrold claims 200 ac in Tryon Co on Bills Cr of Cove Cr; above Stephen Shilton's entry at foot of Young's Mountain; includes his own

Tryon County, NC Land Entries 1778-1779

improvement; entered Jan. 22, 1779; £6.4.

580. granted. George Russel claims 100 ac in Tryon Co on N side of N fork of main Broad R; border: his own land and Goffs Br; entered Jan. 22, 1779; £3.14.

581. granted. George Russel claims 50 ac in Tryon Co on N fork of main Broad R; above his other entry; includes Shadrack Nettles' improvement; entered Jan. 22, 1779; £2.9.

582. granted to Geo Russel. George Russel (write over) claims 100 ac in Tryon Co on main Broad R; between his own land and William Nettles on N side of said river; entered Jan. 22, 1779; £3.14.

583. granted. Baptist Scott claims 600 ac in Tryon Co on S side of Cataba R in Hog pen Bent on said river; border: James Freeman, Saml McCombs, & his own land; entered Jan. 22, 1779; £16.4.

page 122
584. granted. James Logan claims 100 ac in Tryon Co on Beaverdam Cr of First Broad R; border & above: his own land "in" said creek; entered Feb. 1, 1779; £3.14.

585. granted. Thomas Goodbread claims 100 ac in Tryon Co on Durnalds (or Darnalds) Cr on Cove Cr; border: mouth of Plant Br; entered Feb. 1, 1779; £3.14.

586. granted. James Black claims 100 ac in Tryon Co on middle fork of Catheys Cr; border: John Innis and Thomas Donaldson entry; includes his own improvement; entered Feb. 1, 1779; £3.14.

587. granted. George Black claims 100 ac in Tryon Co on Second Broad R; border: his own land on E side; entered Feb. 1, 1779; £3.14.

588. granted to Francis(?) McKemore by order of McMin. Robert McMin claims 100 ac in Tryon Co on both sides of Chestnut Log Br of Sandy Run; border: on upper side of waggon road; includes his own improvement; entered Feb. 3, 1779; £3.14.

page 123
589. granted. Robert McMin claims 100 ac in Tryon Co on head of branch he now lives on on Sandy Run; on both sides of the waggon road; entered Feb. 3, 1779; £3.14.

590. granted. Jeremiah Gage claims 100 ac in Tryon Co on Sandy Run of main Broad R; above ford where Walker's waggon road crosses; includes Mesech Green's improvement; entered Feb. 3, 1779; £3.14.

Tryon County, NC Land Entries 1778-1779

591. granted. Abraham Kuyrkindall claims 50 ac in Tryon Co on Sandy Run of main Broad R; border: his own land he bought from Robert McMin; on both sides of path from Kuyrkindall's to the high shoal; entered Feb. 3, 1779; £2.9.

592. granted. James Shannon claims 200 ac in Tryon Co on branches of Duharts Cr; border: Daniel Gray, William Davis, & Wallace etc; on both sides of path from Shannon's to Logan's; entered Feb. 3, 179; £6.4.

593. discontinued by David Miller Oct. 4, 1779. David Miller claims 150 ac in Tryon Co on Cleghorns Cr of main Broad R; border: Ralph Fleming; border: Feb. 3, 1779; £4.19.

page 124
594. granted. Benjamin Coleclough claim 100 ac in Tryon Co on Cedar Cr of Cove Cr; above Michael McElwrath's at the two forks on said creek; begins near upper ford; entered Feb. 5, 1779; £3.14.

595. granted. Benjamin Coleclough claims 100 ac in Tryon Co on Bills Cr of Cove Cr; below Hendrick's improvement; includes upper shoal on said creek near Bill's Mountain; entered Feb. 5, 1779; £3.14.

596. granted. Benjamin Coleclough claims 50 ac in Tryon Co on waters of main Broad R; border: James Lattas above "his" improvement and includes part thereof; runs round Latas land; entered Feb. 5, 1779; £2.9.

597. granted. Benjamin Coleclough claimsa 50 ac in Tryon Co on Walnut Cr of Green R; border: Waddelton; entered Feb. 5, 1779; £2.9.

598. granted Nov. 9, 1779. George Patterson claims 150 ac in Tryon Co on both sides of Buffeloe Cr; border: William Murphey and his own land; includes a small improvement; entered Feb. 9, 1779; £4.19.

page 125
599. granted. John Lewis claims 150 ac in Tryon Co on waters of Mountain Cr; border: his own land; entered Feb. 12, 1779; £4.19.

600. granted. Elias Allexander claims 50 ac in Tryon Co on N side of main Broad R; border: Thos Dill; higher up river than Dill's; includes Gabriel Clemons' improvement; entered Feb. 12, 1779; £2.9.
601. Elias Allexander claims 200 ac in Tryon Co on Floyds Cr of main Broad R; border: his own land; includes part of the flat rocks; entered Feb. 12, 1779; £6.4.

602. granted. William Dunn claims 100 ac in Tryon Co on waters of upper Camp Cr; border: his own land on W side; entered Feb. 12, 1779; £3.14.

Tryon County, NC Land Entries 1778-1779

603. granted. John McKinney claims 100 ac in Tryon Co on S side of main Broad R; border: his own land on lower line; includes Abraham Clemmons' improvement; entered Feb. 12, 1779; £3.14.

page 126
604. granted. William Cocksey claims 200 ac in Tryon Co on Duncans Br of Second Broad R; border: George Black; includes his own improvement; entered Feb. 12, 1779; £6.4.

605. granted to Wire & Logan. Jas Logan and Robert Wire claims 200 ac in Tryon Co on Suck fork of First Broad R; between Sims' two lines; includes Orson White's improvement; entered Feb. 12, 1779; £6.4.

606. granted to Wire & Logan. Robert Wire and Jas Logan claims 200 ac in Tryon Co on Boreings Br of First Broad R; border: Jeremiah Smith's entry; includes John Boreing's improvement; entered Feb. 12, 1779; £6.4.

607. granted. John Mattox claims 100 (written over 50) ac in Tryon Co on Roaring Run of S fork of Cataba R; border: Robert Gray, Chittam's (or Robert Gray Chittam), his own land, & Loper; entered Feb. 12, 1779; £2.9.

608. granted. Aurthur Monro claims 100 ac in Tryon Co on right hand fork of South Cr of First Broad R; border: Hicory Nut Mountain; includes his own land; entered Feb. 12, 1779; £3.14.

page 127
609. discontinued Aug. 5, 1779 money paid back. Abel Beaty claims 50 ac in Tryon Co on waters of Buffeloe Cr; border: his own land; entered Feb. 19, 1779; £2.9.

610. granted to Nicholas Gozenell. Charles Gozenell claims 100 (written over 50) ac in Tryon Co near or at mouth of Big Long Br; border: George Hovis and Zachariah Spencer and "out from the S fork"; entered Feb. 29, 1779; £2.9.

611. granted to Lewis Lineberger by order of Graham. James Grahams claims 450 ac in Tryon Co on waters of Hoyls Cr of S fork of Cataba R; border: William Anderson, Wm Smith's old place, & Lewis Lineberger; entered Feb. 23, 1779; £12.9.

612. granted to John More. William Smith claims 100 (written over 400) ac in Tryon Co on waters of Duharts Cr; border: McElroy's old place, John More, Jas Shannon, & George Lampkins; includes the Great Lick; entered Feb. 23, 1779; £3.14. (written over 11.4).

613. granted. Stephen Scenter. William Smith claims 100 ac in Tryon Co on Meadow Br of S fork of Cataba R; border: George Lampkin; includes small

Tryon County, NC Land Entries 1778-1779

improvement made by Wm Davis; entered Feb. 23, 1779; £3.14.

page 128
614. granted. Ambrose Foster claims 300 ac in Lincoln (Tryon--lined out) Co on branch of Bridges Br of Crowders Cr; border: John Henry, Allexdr Denney, Andrew Falls, & his own land; entered Mar. 3, 1779; £8.14.

615. granted. James Henderson claims 300 (written over 150) ac in Lincoln (Tryon--lined out) Co near Hoyls Cr; border: Jno More formerly Wm Smith on N side and Jacob Shutley; entered Mar. 3, 1779; £4.19..

616. granted to Jas Logan. Robert Wire and Jas Logan claim 200 ac in Tryon (Lincoln--lined out) Co on W side of Buffeloe Cr; border: Christian Carpenter and Wm Murphey; includes David Robinson's improvement; entered Mar. 3, 1779; £6.4.

617. granted. to Wire; discontinued. Robert Wire and Jas Logan claim 200 ac in Tryon (written over Lincoln) Co on First Broad R; border: Jacob Vangant McElmurry; includes Joseph Gregory's improvement; entered Mar. 3, 1779; £6.4.

618. granted in Miller's name. James Miller and Jas Logan claim 100 ac in Tryon Co on both sides of Green R; border: Dixon; includes McGuire and Isham Hinson's improvement; entered Mar. 9, 1779; £3.14.

page 129
619. granted to Miller. Jas Miller and Jas Logan claims 50 ac in Tryon Co on S side of main Broad R; below John Scott and above Gray; entered Mar. 9, 1779; £2.9.

620. granted. Authur Patterson claims 200 ac in Tryon Co on E side of Buffeloe Cr on heads of Long Br; entered Mar. 9, 1779; £6.4.

621. granted. John McFarland claims 20 ac in Tryon Co being an "Ileand" in Cataba R; below Furasegah (or Turasegah) ford "fornenst" his own land; entered Mar. 9, 1779; £1.14.

622. granted. Thomas Rhine claims 600 ac in Tryon Co on Doctors Cr of Dutchmans Cr of Cataba R; border: Jas Graham, Michael Sides, James Milagan, & his own land; entered Mar. 10, 1779; £16.4.

623. granted. Thomas Rhine claims 400 ac in Tryon Co on waters of Henteys Cr of Cataba R; border: Jas Rutledge, Jas Coburn, & his own land; entered Mar. 10, 1779; £11.4.

page 130

Tryon County, NC Land Entries 1778-1779

624. granted; discontinued Sept. 10, 1783. Charles Gozenell claims 200 ac in Tryon Co on N side of waters of Long Cr; includes waggon road from the court house to Spencer's ford on Bridge Br and Popular Br; entered Mar. 10, 1779; £6.4.

625. granted. Robert Abernathey claims 300 ac in Tryon Co on waters of Jumping Br of Cataba R; border: Robert McCombs, Vincent Cox, & his own land; entered Mar. 10, 1779; £8.14.

626. granted Dec. 9. George Patterson claims 200 ac in Tryon Co on waters of First Broad R; includes Crane's improvement; entered Mar. 10, 1779; £6.4.

627. granted Ramsey & Logan. David Ramsey and Jas Logan claim 200 ac in Tryon Co; border: Wm Ramsey; entered Mar. 10, 1779 £6.4.

628. granted. Peter Carpenter claims 50 ac in Tryon Co on S side of Indian Cr; border: on lower side of John Dillinger and his own land; entered Mar. 12, 1779; £2.9; "due to the publick for this amount 29.15".

page 131
629. granted. Peter Carpenter claims 50 ac in Tryon Co on S side of Indian Cr; border: on upper side of John Dilliner and his own land; entered Mar. 12, 1779; £2.9.

630. granted. Jonathan Gullick and Jas Logan claim 200 (written over 400) ac in Tryon Co on two branches of Sheppords Cr; between Wm Gilbert and Jas Adair; border: side Gilbert on E and S sides; entered Mar. 12, 1779; £6.4 (write over).

631. granted. William Gilbert claims 128 ac in Tryon Co on waters of Sheppards Cr; between and border: Jonathan Gullick, Thomas Morris, & his own land; entered Mar. 12, 1779; £4.8.

632. granted. Thomas Morris claims 200 ac in Tryon Co on waters of Sheppards Cr; border: William Gilbert's late entry on N and his old survey on W side; entered Mar. 13, 1779; £6.4.

633. granted. John McClain claims 100 ac in Tryon Co on Goffs Br of Cove Cr; opposite N corner of Russel's land; includes an old calf pen; entered Mar. 13, 1779; £3.14.

page 132
634. granted. John Smart claims 100 ac in Tryon Co on waters of Cove Cr; border: Allexander McGauhey, Wm Huddlestone, Wm Long, & his own land; entered Mar. 13, 1779; £3.14.

635. granted. Jas Witherow claims 150 ac in Tryon Co on Cane Cr of Broad R;

Tryon County, NC Land Entries 1778-1779

border & between: his own and Saml Andrews surveys; entered Mar. 13, 1779; £4.19.

636. granted Jul. 16; discontinued Nov. 3, 1779. Samuel Elder claims 100 ac in Tryon Co on Cataba R; border: James Beaty, Thomas Robinson, Abraham Scott, & John McFarland; entered Mar. 13, 1779; £3.14.

637. granted to Jese Feathrstone to Merryman Thomas Jan. 1784. George Lampkin claims 640 ac in Tryon Co on waters of S fork of Cataba R; border: Wm Smith sr's entry, Jesse Fetherstone, & Zachariah Spencer; near Hoyl's Mountain; entered Mar. 16, 1779; £17.4.

638. granted. James Holland claims 100 ac in Tryon Co on waters of Little Cataba Cr; border: his own land on N side; entered Mar. 17, 179; £3.14.

page 133
639. granted. William Monday claims 200 ac in Tryon Co on Long Br of Muddy fork of Buffeloe Cr; above Jas Holland's entry on said branch; includes the first large fork and crossings of path from court house to Carson's and path called More's Path; entered Mar. 17, 1779; £6.4.

640. granted to James Foster. Thomas Henderson cliams 200 ac in Tryon Co on waters of Little Cataba Cr; border: on S side of Jas Logan and Job Robinson; entered Mar. 17, 1779; £6.4.

641. granted. Catharine Smith claims 150 ac in Tryon Co on waters of Big Long Cr; border: Jno Pinner and her own land on S side; includes road to Major Hambright's; entered Mar. 17, 1779; £4.19.

642. granted. John Baptist Davis claims 200 ac in Tryon Co on Petsimmon Br of Buffeloe Cr; between Green's old road and ridge path "nearly" includes said road; entered Mar. 25, 1779; £6.4.

643. granted. Jacob Christman claims 100 ac in Tryon Co on First Broad R; border: John McIntire; includes his own improvement; entered Mar. 26, 1779; £2.14.

page 134 [blank page]

page 135
644. granted. William Pailker (or Rilker) claims 200 ac in Tryon Co on waters of Mill Cr of Dutchmans Cr of Cataba R; border: John Con sr, Soloman Sailor, & Thomas Anderson; includes the mill stone; entered Apr. 3, 1779; £6.4.

645. granted. Hugh Shannon claims 50 ac in Tryon Co on waters of Duharts Cr; border: his old and new surveys; entered Apr. 3, 1779; £2.9.

Tryon County, NC Land Entries 1778-1779

646. granted. Jas Holland claims 200 ac in Tryon Co on middle fork of Magness Cr; border: John Altum on W side; entered Apr. 3, 1779; £6.4.

647. granted. Henry Holland claims 200 ac in Tryon Co on Magness Cr; on E side of Wm Jones; entered Apr. 4, 1779; £6.4.

648. granted. George Cox claims 400 ac in Tryon Co on heads of Caney Br; border: Venson Cox, Canady, Cox, & Robert Abernathey; entered Apr. 5, 1779; £11.4.

page 136
649. granted. George Cox claims 200 ac in Tryon Co on W side of Cataba R; border: George Lampkin, Gaskins Scott (or Gaskin and Scott), & Phillips; entered Apr. 5, 1779; £6.4.

650. granted. George Cox claims 60 ac in Tryon Co; border: Lamkin, Rankin, & Kuyrkindall; entered Apr. 5, 1779; £2.9.

651. granted to Hugh Blair. Daniel McCarty (write over) claims 250 (written over 150) ac in Tryon Co on branch of Dutchmans Cr; border: Moses Williams and his own land; entered Apr. 13, 1779; £4.19.

652. granted. Saml Johnson claims 50 ac in Tryon Co on both sides of Dutchmans Cr; border: his own land where he now lives; entered Apr. 13, 1779; £2.19.

653. discontinued by Geo Pea. George Pea claims 200 ac in Tryon Co on waters of Crowders Cr; border: John Henry, Moses Hendry, Ambrose Foster, & his own land; entered Apr. 16, 1779; £6.4.

page 137
654. discontinued by Abraham Scott Sept. 17, 179. Abraham Scott claims 150 ac in Tryon Co on S side of Cataba R; border: Jno McFarland, Jas Beaty, Thomas Robinson, his own land, & the river; entered Apr. 16, 1779; £4.19.

655. granted. Jas Rutledge claims 100 ac in Tryon Co on waters of Dutchmans Cr; border: Jas Coburn and his own land; entered Apr. 20, 1779; £3.14.

656. granted. Robert Lee claims 200 ac in Tryon Co on both sides of Second Broad R; above the high shoals; includes his own improvement; entered Apr. 20, 1779; £6.4.
657. granted. William Cooper claims 100 ac in Tryon Co on E side of Second Broad R; border & below: Robert Lee's entry; entered Apr. 20, 1779; £3.14.

658. granted. Allexander Oar claims 200 ac in Tryon Co on McCashlands Br of

Second Broad R; border: Aaron Deviney and John Walker's entry; includes his own improvement; entered Apr. 20, 1779; £6.4.

page 138
659. granted. Jas Blackburn claims 300 ac in Tryon Co on both sides of branch of Sandy Run; border: Riggs; includes the improvement where he lives; entered Apr. 20, 1779; £8.14.

660. granted. Adam Neil claims 200 ac in Tryon Co on waters of Shoal Run of Muddy fork of Buffeloe Cr; border: Moses More and his own land; entered Apr. 20, 1779; £6.4.

661. granted to John Sloan. John Skrimshire claims 700 (write over) ac in Tryon Co on branch of Buffeloe Cr; border & above: Robert Evires; entered Apr. 20, 1779; £11.4 (8.4--lined out).

662. granted. John Baptist Davis claims 200 ac in Tryon Co on waters of Fitzimon Br of Buffeloe Cr; below his other entry and above John Carruth; entered Apr. 20, 1779; £6.4.

663. granted. Richard Singleton claims 50 ac in Tryon Co on South Cr of First Broad R; border: Stephen Langford, Robert Whitesides, & his own land; includes his own improvemnts; entered Apr. 20, 1779; £2.9.

page 139
664. granted. John Delingar claims 60 ac in Tryon Co on N side of (page torn-- Indian?) Cr; border: John Allexdr, Peter Carpenter, & his own land; includes mouth of Indian Cr; entered Apr. 20, 1779; £2.14.

665. discontinued. Jas Miller claims 500 ac in Tryon Co on E side of Second Broad R; border: John Walker; Wm Henry, & Huddlestone; entered Apr. 20, 1779; £3.14.

666. granted. Samuel Henderson claims 200 ac in Tryon Co on waters of Brushey Cr of Broad R; includes Mathew Potes camp; entered Apr. 20, 1779; £6.4.

667. granted. Jas Henderson claims 10 ac in Lincoln Co; being an island in S fork of Cataba R known as Maple Island; border: his own land; includes his mill house; entered May 1, 1779; £1.9.

668. granted. Jacob Baker claims 100 ac in Lincoln Co on head of Coburns Cr; border: Jas McCarty, Benjamin Armstrong , & his own land; entered May 3, 1779; £3.14.

page 140

669. granted to John Drawn Thremsin (or Skremsin). Peter Duncan claims 150 ac in Lincoln Co on waters of Leapers Cr; border: Richard Jones, Wm Cathey, & Miles Abernathey; includes part of his own improvement; entered May 3, 1779; £3.14.

670. granted. Miles Abernathey claims 300 ac in Lincoln Co on waters of Lepers Cr; border: John Dozer, Robt McCombs, Moses Williams, & Peter Duncan; entered May 3, 1779; £3.14.

671, granted. Joseph Glading claims 100 ac in Lincoln Co on Long Br of Besons Cr; border: his own land; entered May 7, 1779; £3.14.

672. granted. John Mullenix claims 200 ac in Lincoln Co on both sides of Besons Cr; border & above: widow Collins; includes Saml Smith's cabbin; entered May 7, 1779; £6.4.

673. granted. George Cockburn claims 100 ac in Lincoln Co on N side of Besons Cr; on both sides of widow Collins' path; entered May 7, 1779; £3.14.

page 141
674. granted. George Cockburn claims 100 ac in Lincoln Co on S side of Besons Cr; border: his own land and widow Collins; entered May 7, 1779; £3.14.

675. granted. Frederwick (John--lined out) Hambright claims 200 ac in Lincoln Co on Mibines Br on Big Long Cr near Laboon's Mountain; border: tree marked " " above waggon road from Spencer's ford to the court house; entered May 16, 1779; £6.4.

676. to be granted to Robert Alexander & Joseph Henry by Glants' order; granted to John West. Jacob Glants claims 300 ac in Lincoln Co on branches of Doctors Cr; border: Conrad Sailors and "towards" an old waggon road; entered May 16, 1779; £8.14.

677. granted to Jas Henderson by order of Saunders. Richard Saunders claims 200 ac in Lincoln Co on Jumping Br of Big Long Cr; border & above: his own land; entered May 16, 1779; £6.4.

678. granted. William Cathey claims 100 ac in Lincoln Co on Dutchmans Cr or branches thereof; border: John Ramsey, Jno McCarty, Benjamin Armstrong, & Robert Knox; entered May 19, 1779; £3.14.

page 144
679. granted. William Cathey claims 50 ac in Lincoln Co on Cabbin Br of Dutchmans Cr; border: his own land; entered May 20, 1779; £2.9.

680. granted. Christian Money claims 150 ac in Lincoln Co on branches of Long

Lincoln County, NC Land Entries 1779-1780

Cr; border: his own land he bought [from?] Palser Tarter above Tarter's land; entered May 20, 1779; £4.19.

681. granted. Warrick Woodward claims 200 ac in Lincoln Co on waters of Long Cr; border: Nicolass Tarter; below Tarter's land; entered May 20, 1779; £6.4.

682. granted. Joseph Massey claims 200 ac in Lincoln Co on waters of Long Cr; border: Michael Hoyl, Joseph Jenkins, & McCarty's old tract; includes waggon road from Spencer's ford to the court house; entered May 20, 1779; £6.4.

683. granted. Fererwick Rating (or Ratray) claims 200 ac in Lincoln Co on a branch of Crowders Cr; border: Jas Graham's entry; entered May 24, 1779; £6.4.

page 143
684..granted. Ferrard Vanzant sr claims 100 ac in Lincoln Co on S side of S fork of Cataba R; border: Conrod Kinder, Charles Glants, his own land, & the river; entered May 4, 1779; £3.14.

685. granted to Jeremiah Smith's name. Allexander Denney claims 100 ac in Lincoln Co on a small branch of Crowders Cr; border: John Henry, Jas Martin's entry, & his own entry; entered May 25, 1779; £3.14.

686. granted. James Patterson claims 100 ac in Lincoln Co on Duharts Cr; border: his own land; entered May 25, 1779; £3.14.

687. (blank) James Grahams claims 250 ac in Lincoln Co on waters of Walkers Br of Crowders Cr; border or near: Allexdr Gilleland's entry on N side; entered May 26, 1779; £7.9.

688. granted. William Vernor claims 300 ac in Lincoln Co on waters of Little Long Cr; border: land "called" John Low's; includes the Rock Spring; entered May 29, 1779; £8,14,

page 144
689. to be granted to Robert Alexander & Joseph Henry by bargin with Glants; granted to Allexdr. Jacob Glants claims 200 ac in Lincoln Co on Hoyls Cr; border: Josh Hoyl, Lewis Lineberger, & Boston Best jr; entered Jun. 5, 1779; £6.4.

690. granted to John Sloan. John Espey claims 100 ac in Lincoln Co on branch of Crowders Cr; border: Charles McClain "that he sold to Ferguson"; includes Robinson's cabbin; entered Jun. 5, 1779; £3.14.

Lincoln County, NC Land Entries 1779-1780

691. granted. John Cline claims 200 ac in Lincoln Co on branch of Hoyls Cr; border: Lewis Lineberger; includes his own land; entered Jun. 5, 1779; £6.4.

692. granted. William Cogdal claims 200 ac in Lincoln Co on a branch of Long Cr; border: Thomas Perkins and Peter Castner; includes his own improvement; entered Ju. 15, 1779; £6.4.

693. granted. John McGill claims 150 ac in Lincoln Co on S side of Long Cr and on branch of Long Cr; below Costner's field; border: Thos Perkins, Peter Costner, & Geo Peterson; entered Jul. 2, 1779; £4.1.9.

page 145
694. discontinued money returned. Darson Ratclay (or Rackley) claims 100(?) ac in Lincoln Co on waters(?) of Little Cataba Cr; border: N side of Carruth's survey; entered Jul. 2, 1779; £3.14.

695. granted. Darson Racklay claims 200 ac in Lincoln Co on both sides of Little Cataba Cr; border: on S side of Carruth's survey; entered Jul. 2, 1779; £6.4.

696. granted. John Hinner (? faint) claims 150 ac in Lincoln Co on S side of waters of Cataba R; border: on S side of Carruth; entered Jul. 2, 1779; £4.19.

697. granted. Andrew Floyd claims 100 ac in Lincoln Co on waters of Litle Cataba and Duharts Creeks; border: David Elder, Jas McRaynalds, & his own land; entered Jul. 5, 1779; £3.14.

698. granted. David Elder claims 50 ac in Lincoln Co on waters of Duharts Cr; border: Andrew Floid and Jas Paterson; entered Jul. 5, 1779; £2.9.

page 146
699. granted. John Wire claims 50 ac in Lincoln Co on Murpheys Br of Buffeloe Cr; border: his own land; entered Jul. 22, 1779; £2.9.

700. granted. John Skrimshire claims 100 ac in Lincoln Co on Magness Cr of Buffeloe Cr; border: William Monday's entry where "he" now lives; entered Jul. 22, 1779; £3.14.

701. granted. William Graham claims 250 ac in Lincoln Co on both sides of Buffeloe Cr; border: a pine tree marked "W" in forks of a branch below his "plantation" and Jas Collins; entered Jul. 22, 1779; £7.9.

702. discontinued. William Graham claims 100 ac in Lincoln Co; border: a pine tree marked "W" on E side of creek and Jas Collins; includes the bottom and meadow ground left out of Collins' lines; entered Jul. 22, 1779; £3.14.

Lincoln County, NC Land Entries 1779-1780

703. discontinued. Jacob Money and Jas Logan claims 300 ac in Lincoln Co on both sides of Indian Cr; below waggon road from court house to Ramsour's; border: Valentine Money, Thos Black, & Peter Carpenter; entered Aug. 2, 1779; £8.13.

page 147
704. granted. John Titer Beam claims 200 ac in Lincoln Co on Beaverdam Cr of S fork of Cataba R; border: on W side of his land he bought from Benjamin Shaw; entered Aug. 4, 1779; £7.8.

705. granted to John Tucker. John Baptist Davis claim 200 ac in Lincoln Co on waters of Buffeloe Cr; border & between: William Magness and William Jones' surveys; entered Aug. 6, 1779; £7.8.

706. granted. Abel Beaty claims 400 ac in Lincoln Co on both sides of Buffeloe Cr; border: William Magness and his own land; includes a large meadow and low grounds and his own improvement; entered Aug. 6, 1779; £12.8.

707. granted. John Titer Beam claims 250 ac in Lincoln Co on both sides of branch of Beaverdam Cr of S fork of Cataba R; border: his own land; entered Aug. 7, 1779; £8.13.

708. granted. Thomas McGill claims 200 ac in Lincoln Co at head of brancch that runs into Blackwood's field on S side of Long Cr; entered Aug. 9, 1779; £7.8.

page 148
709. granted. Jacob Collins claims 300 ac in Lincoln Co on Lick Br of Buffeloe Cr; border: Jas McAffee and line of the South state; includes Wm Rook's and his own improvement; entered Aug. 10, 1779; £8.13.

710. granted to George Cox by Lamkins' order. George Lampkins jr (written over James F__?__) claims 200 ac in Lincoln Co on a branch of Dutchmans Cr; border: George Lampkins, Wm Magness, & Rutledge; includes Gaskins improvement; entered Aug. 11, 1779; £7.8.
711. granted. Aaron Reily claims 100 ac in Lincoln Co on W side of Buffeloe Cr; border: his other survey "on N and W lines"; entered Aug. 11, 1779; £4.18.

712. granted to Robert Wire. Thomas Parker claims 200 ac in Lincoln Co on Muddy fork of Bufelo Cr; border: Rebecca Caldwell and Jno Tagert; includes "a large flat of meadow land" above Caldwell's land; entered Aug. 20, 1779; £7.8.

713. granted. George Trout claims 200 ac in Lincoln Co on Long Br of Buffalo

Lincoln County, NC Land Entries 1779-1780

Cr; above Robert Wire's entry on fork of said branch; entered Aug. 20, 1779; £7.8,

page 149
714. granted to John Sloan. Robert Brazill claims 150 ac in Lincoln Co at head of Wolf Trap Br of Buffeloe Cr of Broad R; border: John Kirkland on E and S; entered Aug. 25, 1779; £6.3.

715. granted. Stephen Scenter claims 250 ac in Lincoln Co on Wyatts Branches of S fork of Cataba R; on N side of river; border: Jas Scenter sr, Daniel Wiatt, & Jno McKnit Allexdr; entered Aug. 27, 1779; £8.13.

716. granted. James Huggins claims 100 ac in Lincoln Co on waters of Potts Cr; border: his own land on NE side; entered Aug. 27, 1779; £4.18.

717. granted. Jonathan Price (or Davis) claims 150 ac in Lincoln Co on branch of Kings Cr known as Thompson's Cabbin Br; includes Monahan's improvement; entered Sept. 6, 1779; £6.3.

718. granted. Abraham Scott claims 100 ac in Lincoln Co on S side of Cataba R; border: John McFarland, Thos Robinson, & his own land; entered Sept. 17, 1779; £4.18.

page 150
719. granted. Joseph Neil claims 60 ac in Lincoln Co between waters of Mill Cr and Little Cataba R; border: Lofton, Robt Brown, Edward Mellon, & his own land; entered Sept. 18, 1779; £3.18.

720. granted; discontinued Apr. 27, 1780. Stephen Scenter claims 100 ac in Lincoln Co on Bostons (or Broston) Cr; includes vacant land "round" Benjamin Taylor's improvement; entered Sept. 19, 1779; £4.18.

[720A] granted. Stephen Scenter claims 200 (write over) ac in Lincoln Co on Moses Branches; border: Jas Senter, Thos Bohannon, Jno Bohannon, & Joseph Dixon; entered Sept. 19, 1779; £7.18 (write over).

721. granted. Daniel Wiatt claims 300 ac in Lincoln Co on Long Br of Big Ling Cr; border: James Wyatt, Ezekiel Hezlet, Peter Carpenter, & his own land; entered Sept. 20, 1779; £9.18.

722. granted. Feb. 13, 1780. James Rutledge claims 100 ac in Lincoln Co on Dutchmans Cr; border: his own land, Jno Wills, Miles Abernathey, & Jno Walker; entered Sept. 21, 1779; £4.18.

Lincoln County, NC Land Entries 1779-1780

723. granted. James Rutledge claims 40 ac in Lincoln Co on Dutchmans Cr; border: Charles Rutledge, Jno Walker, Wm Cathey, & Moses Williams; entered Sept. 21, 1779; £3.9.

page 151
724. granted. George Lampkins claims [200 faint] ac in Lincoln Co; border: Daniel Wyatt, Edmund Wyatt, Wm Varner(?), & Jas Wyatt; entered Sept. 30, 1779; £3.9.

725. granted. George Patterson claims 100 ac in Lincoln Co on waters of Kings Cr; border: his other entry on N side; higher up than his other entry; entered Oct. 1, 1779; £4.18.

726. granted. Leonard Webb claims 200 ac in Lincoln Co on Lick Br of Coburn Cr of Cataba R; border: John Hill, Wm Morison, Peter Duncan, John Ramsey, John McCartey, & Jacob Baker; includes his own improvmente where he lives; entered Oct. 2, 1779; £7.8.

727. granted. John McCarty claims 200 ac in Lincoln Co on Tanyard Br of Coburns Cr of Cataba R; border: Jacob Baker, Benjamin Armstrong, Wm Cathey, John Ramsey, & Leonard Webb's entry; includes his own improvement; entered Oct. 2, 1779; £7.8.
728. granted. Samuel McMin claims 150 ac in Lincoln Co on W side of Cataba R on waters of Seigles Cr; border: Abraham Wamock, Thomas Beaty, Sceiglas, & his own land; entered Oct. 3, 1779; £6.3.

page 152
729. discontinued Mar. 20, 1780. James Henderson claims 400 ac in Lincoln Co on both sides of Buffelo Cr; includes road from Benjamin Harding's to Warlock's Mill; includes a shoal and large flat of meadow on said creek; entered Oct. 14, 1779; £12.8.

730. granted to Saml Dyer. Edward Cornwall claims 60 ac in Lincoln Co on Potts Cr of Buffelo Cr; border: Soloman Beson, Jas Huggins, & his own land; entered Oct. 19, 1779; £3.18.

731. granted. Preston Goforth claims 250 ac in Lincoln Co on both sides of Besons Cr; border: Soloman Beson and Edward Cornwall; includes his own improvement; entered Oct. 19, 1779; £3.13.

732. granted. Samuel Collins claims 60 ac in Lincoln Co on both sides of Besons Cr; border: Preston Goforth's entry #731 on W side; entered Oct. 19, 1779; £3.18.

Lincoln County, NC Land Entries 1779-1780

733. granted. Christopher Monday claims 200 ac in Lincoln Co between waters of Beaverdam and Long Branches; "nearly to" Wm Monday's entry on E side; includes Polly's old road; entered Oct. 19, 1779; £7.9.

page 153
734. granted. John Trout claims 200 ac in Lincoln Co on Popular Spring Br of Long Br of Buffelo Cr; border: Robert Wire and George Trout; entered Oct. 23, 1779; £7.8.

735. caveated 50(?) ac of Wells' claimed by Aurthur Patterson Nov. 9, 1779. John Wells claims 100 ac in Lincoln Co on S side of waters of Kings Cr; border: Arthur Patterson and his own land; entered Oct. 18, 1779; £4.18.

736. granted. John Beasour claims 150 ac in Lincoln Co on N fork of Kittle Cr of S fork of Cataba R; border: George Beasour, Peter Laboon, & John Carpenter; entered Oct. 30, 1779; £6.3.

737. granted. Andrew Hoiles claims 100 ac in Lincoln Co on N side of S fork of Cataba R; border: Christian Rhodes, Boston Best, his own land, & Michael Hoyles; entered Oct. 30, 1779; £4.18.

738. granted. Daniel Wyatt claims 200 ac in Lincoln Co on Long Br of Big Long Cr; border: Edmund Wyatt, Ezekiel Hezlet, & his own land; entered Nov. 1, 1779; £7.8.

page 154
739. entered by John Wells sr #735. Arthur Patterson claims 50 ac in Lincoln Co on S side of Kings Cr; border: on S corner of his own land where he now lives; entered Nov. 3, 1779; £3.13.

740. granted. John Gullick claims 100 ac in Lincoln Co on N side of Little Cattaba Cr; border & between: his own [land] and Berry; entered Nov. 9, 1779; £4.18.

741. granted. John Gullick claims 100 ac in Lincoln Co on both sides of Little Cataba Cr; border: Jno Gullick sr and Saml Jingles; entered Nov. 9, 1779; £4.18.

742. granted. Jacob McFarlin claims 150 ac in Lincoln Co on N branches of Kings Cr; border: Simon Kuyrkindall and Aurthur Featherstone; entered Nov. 11, 1779; £5.13.

743. granted. Edward Cornwall claims 200 ac in Lincoln Co on waters between Crowders Cr and Kings Cr; includes crossings of road from Beson's to Harmon's (or Hamon's); entered Nov. 11, 1779; £7.8.

Lincoln County, NC Land Entries 1779-1780

page 155
744. granted. Richard Saunders claims 50 ac in Lincoln Co on head of Vernors Br of Crowders Cr; on S side of the mountain; entered Nov. 11, 1779; £3.13.

745. granted. Jonathan Heager claims 100 ac in Lincoln Co on waters of Killians Cr; border: Henry Huver and Fawning; entered Nov. 20, 1779; £4.18.

746. granted. Nicholas Friday claims 200 ac in Lincoln Co on N side of Dillingers Cr on Hog Br; border: Henry Dillinger on N side; entered Nov. 23, 1779; £7.8.

747. granted. Nicholas Friday claims 200 ac in Lincoln Co on branch on S side of Dillingers Cr; below & nearly joins Arney; entered Nov. 23, 1779; £7.8.

748. granted. John Sloan claims 50 ac in Lincoln Co on waters of Muddy fork of Buffelo Cr; border: his own land; includes his spring and spring house; entered Dec. 7, 1779; £3.13.

page 156
749. granted John Sloan claims 200 ac in Lincoln Co on Persimmon Br; above Carruth's land; includes a pine marked "IS"; entered Dec. 7, 1779; £7.8.

750. granted. Allexander More claims 150 ac in Lincoln Co on waters of Hoyls Cr; border: Lewis Lineberger, Boston Best jr, & his own land on W side; entered Dec. 18, 1779; £6.3.

751. granted to Thomas Parker. Joseph Nicols claims 200 ac in Lincoln Co on waters of Muddy fork of Buffelo Cr; border: widow Caldwell and Thomas Parker's entry on W side; entered Dec. 20, 1779; £7.8.

752. granted. Thomas Parker claims 250 ac in Lincoln Co on head of Magness Br and branch that runs into Muddy fork; includes Murphey's road and McAfee's pond; entered Dec. 20, 1779; £8.13.

753. granted. George Lampkins claims 150 ac in Lincoln Co; border: Robert Johnson's S line on head of "his" spring branch and Rudasail; entered Dec. 30, 1779; £6.3.

754. granted. George Lampkin sr claims 150 ac in Lincoln Co on both sides of Keeners Br; border: Robert Johnson's W line; entered Dec. 30, 1779; £6.3.

755. granted. Archibald Alison claims 100 ac in Lincoln Co on waters of N fork of Crowder (? faint) Cr; border: Ferguson, John Oats, & Peter Harmon; includes

Lincoln County, NC Land Entries 1779-1780

where Robinson had a smith shop; entered Jan. 17, 1780; £4.18.

756. granted. Saml Monday claims 100 ac in Lincoln Co on Long Br of Muddy fork of Buffelo Cr; border: John Holland's entry on lower end; entered Jan. 20, 1780; £4.13.

757. granted. Frances Hanbay claims 150 ac in Lincoln Co on Long Br; between William Monday and widow Caldwell and joins widow Caldwell; entered Jan. 20, 1780; £6.3.

758. granted. William Morris claims 100 ac in Lincoln Co on Besons Cr; border & below: Cockburn; entered Jan. 20, 1780; £4.13.

page 158
759. granted. James Johnson claims 50 ac in Lincoln Co; border: William Nance; Duhard's old line (or William Nance Dunhard), & Joseph Scott; entered Jan. 20, 1780; £3.13.

760. granted. Robert Abernathey claims 150 ac in Lincoln Co on waters of Jumping Br; border: Vinson Cox and his own land; entered Jan. 20, 1780; £6.3.

761. granted. Miles Abernathey claims 100 ac in Lincoln Co; border: John Walker (or Watkins), Wm Cathey's old place, & land he bought from Richard Jones; entered Jan. 20, 1780; £4.18.

762. granted to Allexander same (or Saml). Robert Allexander and Joseph Henry claim 150 ac in Lincoln Co on Hoyls Cr of South Fork; border: Boston Best jr and Christian Rhodes; entered Jan. 20, 1780; £6.8.

763. granted. Boston Best jr claims 150 ac in Lincoln Co on N side of S fork of Cataba R on Lick Br; border: his old patent line, his new entry, & John Hoyl; entered Jan. 22, 1780; £6.8.
END OF BOOK

Index to Tryon & Lincoln Co Land Entries 1779-1780

Abernathey, David   240
Abernathey, Miles   669, 670, 722, 761
Abernathey, Robert   625, 648, 760
Adair, Jas   630
Adkins, Henry   409
Alderidge, Nathaniel   4, 5, 278
Aldridge, Jas   278
Allexander, Abraham   2
Allexander, Elias   184, 249, 600, 601
Allexander, John   457, 465, 544, 545, 664
Allexander, John McK   23, 78, 249, 259, 316, 362, 715
Alexander (Alexander), Robert   329, 409, 676, 689, 762
Allison (Alison), Archibald   755
Allison, Robert   140, 183
Alson,   194
Alston,   350, 409, 412
Alston, Wm   38
Altum, John   646
Anches,   76
Anderson, James   334
Anderson, John   24, 25, 516
Anderson, Thomas   644
Anderson, William   611
Andrew, Saml   145
Andrews, Saml   635
Armstrong,   423
Armstrong, Benjamin   668, 678, 727
Armstrong, Francis   178, 181
Armstrong, James   462
Armstrong, James jr   576
Armstrong, John   163, 181
Armstrong, William   337, 568
Armstrong, William jr   134, 476, 576
Armstrong, Wm sr   576
Arney,   747
Arnold,   211
Arrington, Thomas   230

Ashley, John   321
Aspey, Saml   317
Auston,   421
Auston, John   384
Baker, Jacob   668, 726, 727
Baker, William   470, 521
Baldridge,   240
Baldridge, Allexander   555
Balshos, John   54
Bar,   106, 388
Barges, Joseph   494
Barkly, Robt   275
Barnet,   153
Barnet, Abraham   540
Barry, Richard   249
Bary, Hugh   64
Basset, William   195
Bates,   155
Bathley, George   89
Beam, John T   704, 707
Beard,   331, 403, 548
Beard, Adamey   42
Beard, James   2
Beard (Baird), Joe   48
Beard (Baird), John   12, 42, 60, 312, 343, 454
Beard, John jr   59, 279
Beard (Baird), William   12, 313
Beasour, George   444, 736
Beasour, John   736
Beaty,   266, 441, 530
Beaty, Abel (Able)   82, 274, 275, 306, 339, 439, 609
Beaty, Adam   706
Beaty, Deborah   74, 325
Beaty, Frances   74, 170
Beaty, Hugh   356
Beaty, James   198, 636
Beaty, Jas   471, 654
Beaty, Joseph   163, 178. 181
Beaty, Thomas   82, 306, 728
Beaty, Wallace   170, 323, 356
Beaty, William   306
Beaverns, Joseph   288
Bedford,   562

Index to Tryon & Lincoln Co Land Entries 1779-1780

Bedford, James   195
Bedford, Jonas   144, 213, 214, 250, 251, 252, 253, 254, 255, 256, 257, 258, 280, 281, 365-369, 435, 481, 484
Bedford, Raymond   367
Bent, Hog pen   583
Berry,   313, 349, 523, 740
Berry, Hugh   2, 64
Berry, William   54, 474
Beson,   743
Beson, Soloman   56, 303, 327, 730, 731
Best, Boston   8, 157, 737
Best, Boston jr   8, 689, 751, 762, 763
Best, Boston sr   193
Biggerstaff, Aaron   391
Biggerstaff, Benjamin   337
Biggerstaff, Samuel   33
Biggs,   92
Black, George   587, 604
Black, James   565, 586
Black, John   535
Black, Thomas   436, 733
Blackburn, Jas   659
Blackburn, Samuel   546, 547
Blackwell, Daniel   433
Blackwood,   318, 708
Blair, Hugh   651
Blankenship, Isam   340
Blankinship, John   556
Blanton, George   308
Boaty, Francis   62
Boaty, Wallace   62
Bohannon, Thos   720A
Bolinger, John   315
Booth, William   232
Boreing, John   606
Boreing, Joseph   308
Borinss, Charles   466A
Bracket,   214
Bradley, James   90
Bradley, Joseph   553
Carpenter, Peter   233, 235, 437, 438, 452, 458, 628,

Bradly, Jas   247
Brazill, Robert   714
Bridges, Benjamin   78
Bridges, Moses   75, 517
Bridget, William   209
Briggs, Gray   485
Brison, John   54
Brothers, Thomas   269
Brown, Mathew Brown   12
Brown, Robt   719
Buchannon, John   23
Buchannon, Thomas   23
Buntin, William   398
Burgess, Joseph   473
Burke Co, NC   346, 554
Burnet, Joseph   115
Burnet, Josua   510
Burnet, Thomas   113, 114
Butter, Walter   400
Byers, William   506
Caldwell, Rebecca   712
Caldwell, Samuel   64
Caldwell, widow   19, 338, 751, 757
Camp,   509
Camp, Benjamin   512
Camp, James   361, 392
Camp, John   360, 362, 370
Camp, Joseph   308, 570
Camp, Nathan   511, 513
Camp, Thomas   507, 508, 509, 516
Camp, William   269
Campbell, Thomas   243, 278
Camphil, Frances   55
Canady,   648
Cancellor, Philip   316
Capshaw,   310
Capshaw, Essex   420
Capshaw, James   398, 407
Capshaw, William   472
Carpenter, Christian   18, 177, 616
Carpenter, John   307, 736, 629, 665, 703, 721
Carruth,   6, 324, 694, 695,

Index to Tryon & Lincoln Co Land Entries 1779-1780

696, 749
Carruth, Adam   431
Carruth, John   14, 76, 236, 662
Carson,   232, 271, 464, 639
Carson, James   465
Carson, John   34
Castle, Elisha H   465, 486
Castner, Peter   318, 692
Cathey,   208
Cathey, George jr   157
Cathey, William   669, 678, 679, 723, 727, 761
Chittam,   607
Chittam, John   163, 181
Chittem,   178
Christman, Jacob   643
Chronicle, William   51, 267, 268
Clark, Abraham   84, 169, 176
Clark, Joseph   574
Clark, Nicolas   573
Clayton, Phineas   232, 327
Cleghorne, widow   387
Clemmons, Abraham   603
Clemons, Gabriel   600
Cline, John   691
Clinton, Robert   470
Cloninger, Adam   569
Cobb, Ambrose   32, 202, 333
Coborn, James   44
Coburn, Jas   623, 655
Cockburn,   758
Cockburn, Goerge   84, 673, 674
Cocks, David   531
Cocksey, William   604
Cogdal, William   692
Cokerhom, Mina   413
Cokerhom, Phillip   412, 413
Coleclough, Benjamin   548, 594, 595, 596, 597
Collenwood,   221
Collins, Jacob   709
Collins, James   150, 701, 702

Collins, John   77, 169, 292, 298
Collins, Pheby   169
Collins, Samuel   150, 175, 732
Collins, Samuel jr   150
Collins, widow   84, 672, 673, 674
Collins, William   449
Con, John sr   644
Conaway,   397
Connel, Jacob   205, 297
Cooper, William   657
Cornwall, Edward   730, 731, 743
Costner, Peter   693
Couller, Allexander   186A
Coulter, Allexander   52, 207, 299, 538
Cowen, John   555
Cowsar, John   446
Cox,   648
Cox, George   648, 649, 650, 710
Cox, Venson   648
Cox, Vincent   625
Cox, Vinson   760
Crane,   626
Crawford, John   403
Crow, James   174
Cummins, John   166, 415
Cuningham, James   51, 198
Cunningham, James   53
Curruth, Adam   189, 190, 222
Curruth, John   191
Curruth, Robert   68
Dalley, James   325
Daugherty, Richard   445
Daves, William   467
Davidson, Allexdr   293, 517
Davis, William   592
Davis, George   168, 182, 397, 405, 421
Davis, Henry   172
Davis, John B   85, 642, 705
Davis, John D   662
Davis, Jonathan   717

Index to Tryon & Lincoln Co Land Entries 1779-1780

Davis, Joseph   311
Davis, William   312, 331, 613
Deal, George   13
Denney, Allexander   614, 685
Dever, John   529
Deviney, Aaron   341, 658
Dickey, David   120, 387
Dickey, James   378, 564
Dickson, Joseph   267
Dickson, Thos   276
Dicky, Anthony   100
Dicky, George   117
Dilbeck, John   440
Dill, Thos   600
Dillinger, Henry   746
Dillinger (Delinger), John   457, 458, 628, 629, 664
Dills, Peter   435
Dinnard, John   328
Dixon,   618
Dixon, Joseph   17, 70, 326, 720A
Dixon, Thos   563
Dollom,   421
Dozer, John   670
Donaldson, Thomas   565, 586
Douglas, Martha   551
Dover, John   172
Drues,   268
Duckey, David   349
Dudderod, John   39
Dudderow, John   134
Duff, Denis   227
Duhard,   759
Duhard, William N   759
Duhart, James   2
Dukey, George   345
Duly, Henry   282, 283
Dunaway, Samuel   235
Duncan, Peter   669, 670, 726
Dunn,   284
Dunn, William   602
Foster, Ambrose   29, 575, 614, 653
Foster, James   640
Fouch, Jonathan   225

Dyer, Saml   730
Eaves, William   382
Edwards, Robert   401
Elder, David   265, 697, 698
Elder, Samuel   198, 636
Elkins, Shadrach   481
Ellis, James   503
Ensley, John   34, 463, 464, 465
Ensly, John   33
Erwin, Hugh   432
Espey, John   690
Espey, Samuel   151
Espey (Espy), Thomas   27, 47, 222, 317
Eve, William   105
Evires, Robert   661
Falls,   5
Falls, Andrew   614
Falls, Gilbreath   177
Farmers,   216
Fastece, Thomas   72
Fawning,   31, 745
Featherstone, Aurthur   742
Feindergerrard, Conrod   39
Fergus, John   241, 270, 271, 327
Ferguson, (Forguson),   690, 755
Ferguson, Andrew   40
Ferguson, Moses   28
Ferguson, Robert   28, 180
Fetherstone, Jesse   637
Findley, Robert   65
Fisher, John   502
Fisher, Nicholas   501
Flack, John   533, 534
Fleming, George   532
Fleming, Ralph   593
Fleming, Richard   470
Floyd, Andrew   697, 698
Folly, John N   229
Frances, Edward   304
Freeman, James   583
French, Samuel   104, 397
Friday, Nicholas   576, 746,

Index to Tryon & Lincoln Co Land Entries 1779-1780

747
Frout, George 16
Gage, Daniel 521
Gage, David 216
Gage, Jeremiah 590
Gardiner, William 231
Gaskins, 649, 710
George, David 345
Gerrard, Conrod T 39
Gerry, 55
Ghant, Thomas 44
Gilbert, 122
Gilbert, William 91, 106, 109, 200, 201, 335, 388, 389, 391, 630, 631, 632
Gilbreath, Joseph 267
Gilleland, Allexdr 179, 687
Gillespie, 58
Gillespie, John 9
Gilmore, Frances 9
Glading, Joseph 67, 69, 79, 156, 239, 529, 671
Glant, Frederwick 235
Glants, Charles F 39
Glants, Charles 684
Glants, Jacob 39, 676, 689
Glding, Joseph 46
Goff, John 111
Goforth, Preston 731, 732
Goings, William 436
Goodbread, John 138
Goodbread, Phillip 93, 93A, 138, 535
Goodbread, Thomas 585
Gorman, John 234
Gozenell, Charles 610, 624
Gozenell, Nicholas 610
Graham, 154
Graham, James 44, 179, 611, 622, 683, 687
Graham, William 159, 166, 217, 218, 462, 701, 702
Grant, William 477
Gray, 197, 619
Gray, Daniel 234, 276, 312, 592

Gray, Robert 471, 607
Gray, William 103
Graydec, 85
Grayson, Joseph 554
Greans, Thomas 209
Green, 562
Green, Abednego 455
Green, Jervis 411
Green, Mesech 590
Gregory, Absalem 224
Gregory, Jonathan 242, 322
Gregory, Joseph 442, 617
Groves, William 575
Gryder, Martin 86
Gullick, John 49, 740, 741
Gullick, John jr 472
Gullick, Jonathan 65, 326, 347, 350, 418, 424, 426, 427, 630, 631
Guthery, 293
Guthery, Frances 271
Guthery, Mathew 287, 516
Hagerty, William 334
Haggins, John jr 42
Hagins, John 42
Hain, Joseph 61
Hais, Samuel 295, 386
Hall, William 219, 487, 489, 494
Hambright, Frederwick 134, 158, 190, 436, 675
Hambright, Major 248, 641
Hamelton, Charles 223
Hamilton, William 136
Hamon, 743
Hampton, 351, 396
Hampton, Andrew 105, 549, 550
Hampton, Edward 83, 439
Hampton, Major 385
Hanbay, Frances 757
Hane, 421
Harce, 421
Harding (Hardin), 271, 464
Harding, Benjamin 77, 147, 270, 309, 504, 729

Index to Tryon & Lincoln Co Land Entries 1779-1780

Harding, Benjamin jr 298
Harding, David 170, 298, 537
Harding (Hardin), Jonathan 170, 174, 495, 524, 537
Harding, Joseph 309
Harmon, 743
Harmon, Peter 755
Harmon, Wm 378
Harris, George 230
Harris, John 21
Harris, Wm 560
Harrison, 567
Harrold, Isaac 579
Hawkins, Michael 414
Hawkins (Hawkens), Thomas 37, 438, 452
Hawkins, William 435
Hazlet, Ezekiel 10, 11
Heager, Jonathan 745
Hedigh, Andrew 220
Hedley, John 483
Heigh, Andrew 316
Hein, Philip 57, 272, 330
Hein, Robert 330
Henderson, James 3, 9, 43, 615, 667, 677, 729
Henderson, Nathaniel 2
Henderson, Richard 360, 361
Henderson, Samuel 666
Henderson, Thomas 248, 640
Henderson, William 189
Hendrey, John 29
Hendrick, 595
Hendricks, John 282, 283
Hendricks, Saml 577
Hendry, Moses 13, 29, 653
Hendry, Thomas 43, 53, 273
Henry, John 614, 685
Henry, Joseph 347, 350, 382, 383, 409, 410, 455, 653,
Horton, 452
Horton, George 37
Hostaller, Adam 31
Hostatler, John 57
Hostatler (Hostaller), Mical 149, 177
676, 689, 762
Henry, Wm 665
Henson, 186
Herod, Thomas 454
Heron, Denis 296
Hezlep, Andrew 33, 34, 442
Hezlet, Ezekiel 437, 451, 721, 738
Hicks, James 433
Hicks, Richard 184, 480
Hicks, Thomas 152
Hider, Benjamin 352
Hightower, John 171
Hilhouse, James 324
Hill, 360
Hill, Able (Abel) 286, 450
Hill, John 726
Hillhouse, James 6, 7, 199, 321
Hinner, John 696
Hinnis, 168
Hinson, Allen 417
Hinson, Allon 538
Hinson, Isham 618
Hogan (Hogans), Christian 498
Hogan, Daniel 183
Hogan (Hogans), Edward 161, 295, 498
Hoiles, Andrew 737
Holaway, Robert 231
Holder, Edward 472
Holland, Henry 647
Holland, Isaac 49, 65
Holland (Hollan), James 137, 153, 230, 231, 383, 571, 638, 639, 646
Holland, John 232, 248, 756
Hooper, 429
Hops, John 38
Hosteller, John 28, 204
Hover, Henry 745
Hover, Soloman 132
Hovis, George 610
Howard, 108
Hoyl, 6, 11

Index to Tryon & Lincoln Co Land Entries 1779-1780

Hoyl, John   8, 22, 226, 319, 460, 763
Hoyl, Josh   689
Hoyl, Martin   10
Hoyl (Hoyles), Michael   318, 444, 459, 682, 737
Huddleston, James   342
Huddleston, William   102
Huddlestone,   665
Huddlestone, David   341, 342
Huddlestone, William   135, 336, 634
Huen, James   102
Huey, James   135, 336
Huggins,   59
Huggins, James   56, 61, 716, 730
Huggins, John   64, 90, 134, 139
Huggins, John jr   89, 332
Huggins, John sr   332
Humpreys, William   514
Husdbery, John   303
Huselbery, John   303
Hutson,   406, 422
Hydar, Benjamin   475
Iec, Jno   245
Innis, John   586
Irving, James   125
Jackson, John   300
Jasper, Henry   314
Jenkins,   474
Jenkins, David   233
Jenkins, Edward   233, 438, 452
Jenkins, Hugh   32, 44, 173, 202, 203
Jenkins, James   203
Jenkins, Joseph   158. 682
Jingles, Saml   741
Johnson,   394
Johnson, Benjamin   218
Johnson, James   759
Johnson, Jesse   48
Johnson, Robert   753, 754
Johnson, Samuel   32, 202, 652

Johnson, William   512
Johnson, William C   572
Jones, John   316, 379
Jones, Richard   669, 761
Jones, Sep   426
Jones, Walter   79
Jones, William   647, 705
Jostice, Thomas   478
Julian, Samuel   232
Justice, Thomas   399
Kalliak, Jon   2
Kanady, Edmond   519
Kawkins, Phelimon   435
Keithrow, John   135
Keller, Andrew   177
Kelly, Henry   98
Kerr, Nathaniel   356
Kersey, Randolph (Randolf)   488, 490, 491
Killian,   203
Kilpatrick, Joseph   50
Kimbol, Isaac   486
Kinder, Conrod   684
King, Barnet   369
King, Barney   144
Kirkland, John   714
Kitchisides, James   434
Knox, Robert   678
Kuyrkindal, Capt   368
Kuyrkindall (Kirkonel),   213, 521, 650
Kuyrkindall, Abraham   285, 286, 434, 511, 591
Kuyrkindall (Kuyrkonel, Kerkonel), John   124, 337, 357, 402, 536
Kuyrkindall (Kirkindal), Simon   205, 742
Laboon, Allexander   444
Laboon, Peter   444, 543, 736
Lampkin (Lamkin),   650
Lampkin (Lamkin), George   3, 43, 234, 612, 613, 637, 649, 710, 724, 753
Lampkin (Lamkin), George jr   276, 710

Index to Tryon & Lincoln Co Land Entries 1779-1780

Lampkin, George sr   754
Lampkin, Uel   309
Lampkin, W C   309
Langford, Stephen   210, 211, 254, 663
Langham,   536
Largent, James   111, 347
Latling, James   344
Lattas, James   596
Laughter,   377
Ledbeatter, George   527
Ledbetter, Richard   291
Lee, Gash   572
Lee, Robert   656, 657
Leeper, Nicholas   288
Leper,   471
Leper, Nicolas   559
Lewis, David   141, 143, 375, 376, 380, 531
Lewis, James   55
Lewis, John   599
Licklogs, M Moree   70
Liles,   365
Liles, David   280, 363, 448
Lindsey, Benjamin   563
Lineberger, Lewis   8, 37, 158, 611, 689, 691, 750
Linn, James   208
Little,   235
Little, John   141
Lively,   251, 255, 268
Lofton,   719
Lofton, Saml   55
Logan,   334, 592
Logan, James   35, 36, 95, 164, 165, 166, 212, 310, 311, 390, 420, 421, 425-431, 480, 483, 492, 496, 523, 584,
McCarroll, Nathaniel   35, 36, 92
McCarter, William   244
McCarty,   682
McCarty, Cornelius   22
McCarty, Daniel   651
McCarty, Jas   668
McCarty (McCartey), John   605, 606, 616-619, 630, 640, 703
Logan, John   146, 160
Logan, Joseph   441
Logan, William   160, 552
Long, Wm   634
Losan, James jr   310A
Low,   459
Low, John   688
Lowry,   337
Lozar, Jas   1
Lusk, John   238, 247, 264
Lusk, William   374
Mackey, Allexander   108, 142, 143, 376, 380, 408, 542
Magness,   323
Magness, James   224
Magness, John   86
Magness, Joseph   312
Magness, Perry G   86
Magness, Perry G jr   62, 67, 79, 88, 225, 302
Magness, Perry G sr   80, 81, 85
Magness, Perygren sr   62
Magness, William   14, 15, 274, 566, 705, 706, 710
Margane,   111
Martin, George   437
Martin, James   223, 685
Masons, William   41
Massey, Joseph   682
Massey, William   7, 10, 197
Matok, John   471
Mattox, John   178, 607
McAfee,   752
McAfee (McAffee), James   289, 709, 678, 726, 727
McCashland,   114
McCashland, Robert   220
McClain, Charles   690
McClain (McClaine, McClane), John   117, 344, 373, 403, 633
McClain, John jr   456

Index to Tryon & Lincoln Co Land Entries 1779-1780

McClain, John sr   454, 455
McClean,   475
McClure, John   43, 50, 52, 53, 522
McCombs, Robert   625, 670
McCombs, Saml   583
McCormick, Thomas   131, 132
McDaniel, Joseph   282, 295, 301, 386, 406, 407, 422
McDonald,   381
McDonald, Allexander   119
McDonald, Jeremiah   381
McDowell, Charles   260
McElmurry, Jacob V   617
McElroy,   612
McElwrath, Michael   557, 558, 594
McFadden,   219
McFadden, Allexandr   352
McFadden, James   374
McFadden, John   343, 344, 352, 373, 377, 403
McFarland, James   353
McFarland, John   30, 329, 575, 621, 636, 654, 718
McFarlen, James   478
McFarlin, Jacob   742
McGahey, William   536
McGauhey, Allexander   634
McGill, John   693
McGill, Thomas   708
McGowen, William   152
McGuire,   618
McIntire, Allexander   242, 493, 495
McIntire, John   340, 643
McIntyre, Alexander   171
McKealy, John   476
McKemore, Francis   588
McKinney,   322
McKinney, John   122, 245, 469, 603
McKinney, William   340
McKinsey, William   193
McLean, Charles   140, 151
McMin, Robert   588, 589, 591
McMin, Samuel   728
McNealy,   477
McRaynalds, Jas   697
Measonatt, Joseph   120
Medlock, Charles   195, 284
Mellon, Edward   719
Melone, Robert   106, 116, 355
Metcaf, Anthony   161, 162
Miligan (Milagan), James   461, 622
Miller,   284
Miller, David   1, 13, 20, 445, 446, 562, 567, 593
Miller, James   35, 36, 50, 92, 93, 95, 103, 109, 182, 185, 200, 201, 446, 564, 617, 619, 665
Miller, James jr   192, 261, 262, 263
Miller, James sr   522, 523
Miller, Robert   313
Mills, Ambrose   162, 489
Mills, William   142, 206, 215, 491
Mills, William jr   487
Mills, Wm sr   489
Mitchell, Robert   459
Mode, James   242
Moffit, John   237
Monahan,   717
Monday, Christopher   733
Monday, Saml   756
Monday, William   339, 639, 700, 733, 757
Mondy, Valentine   703
Money, Chrisly   137
Money, Christian   18, 19, 177, 439, 680
Money, Jacob   19, 58, 66, 703
Monro, Aurthur   608
Mony, Jacob   18
Moor, Samuel   559
More, Aaron   458
More, Allexander   750, 243
More, John   133, 136, 186, 187, 188, 246, 612, 615

Index to Tryon & Lincoln Co Land Entries 1779-1780

More, Joseph 52, 215
More, Moses 127, 137, 660
More, William 133, 267, 461, 473
More, William jr 246
Morison, Wm 84, 486, 726
Morris, James 527
Morris, Thomas 96, 107, 346, 348, 631, 632
Morris, William 176, 515, 758
Mosely, Robert 354
Mostiller, Peter 66
Mullenix, John 672
Murphey, 46, 464, 752
Murphey, William 598, 616
Muzick, Abraham 143, 394
Muzick, George 408
Muzick, John 395
Nance, William 759
Neil, 325
Neil, Adam 71, 148, 465, 660
Neil (Neal), Andrew 149, 177
Neil, Joseph 55, 719
Nelson, Andrew 294
Nettles (Neetles), Shadrack 550, 581
Nettles, William 118, 577, 578, 592
Norman, Forney G 483
Norman, Thomas 278, 313
Norton, 158
Oar, Allexander 658
Oats, John 755
Oneal, Jonathan 401
Orman, Benjamin 26, 27
Polk, John 24, 25
Polk, Thos 267
Polly, 733
Polly, James 16, 17, 539, 540
Pool, William 296
Poor, Andrew 482
Porter, David 468
Porter, William 305, 467
Potes, John 130
Potes, Mathew 666

Orman, James 26
Otries, Absolem 230
Owen, John 542
Owens, Mosely 448
Ozburn, Adlai 492
Ozburn, Michael 359
Pailker, William 644
Pain, John 572
Palmer, George 452, 453, 459
Paris, George 167
Parker, Thomas 338, 712, 751, 752
Parker, Wm 552
Pate, Matthew 136
Paterson, 156
Paterson, Jas 698
Paterson, Mathew 536
Patrick, Andrew 49, 65
Patterson, Allexander 65
Patterson, Arthur (Authur) 620, 735, 739
Patterson, George 314, 598, 626, 725
Patterson, James 41, 686
Pea, George 29, 653
Perkins, Thomas 692, 693
Peterson, Geo 693
Phillips, 649
Phillips, David 320, 333
Phipher, Jno 206
Picerell, 345
Pinner, John 199, 641
Plank, Jacob 222
Plank, Peter 222
Plunket, Christopher 485
Polk, 461
Pots, Jonathan 61
Potter, Thomas 561
Potts, George 469
Potts, John 107, 290, 291, 348, 476, 534
Potts, Mary 291
Price, Jonathan 717
Priggs, 92
Prockter, Nathan 208
Queen, 542

Index to Tryon & Lincoln Co Land Entries 1779-1780

Queen, Hugh 188, 551, 552
Queen, Peter 423
Quinn, 479
Rackley, Darson 694, 695
Ramsey, 462
Ramsey, David 315, 627
Ramsey, John 678, 726, 727
Ramsey, Wm 627
Ramsour, 703
Rankin, 650
Rankin, Samuel 569
Rannolds, Thomas 519
Ratclay, Darson 694
Rating, Fererwick 683
Ratray, Fererwick 683
Reavis, Isham 377, 378, 379, 393, 396
Redy, Aaron 177
Reed, 11
Reily, 399
Reily (Reiley, Riely), Aaron 73, 83, 95A, 122, 325, 388, 404, 419, 439, 711
Russel, 633
Reves, Isham 488
Rhine, Jacob 22
Rhine, Thomas 622, 623
Rhodes, Christian 737, 762
Rhods, Jacob 38
Rice, Isaac 524, 528
Rice, Moses 528
Rice, William 278, 279
Richardson, 433
Richardson, Samuel 485
Richerds, John 90, 501, 502
Richesides, James 368
Riggs, 216, 659
Riggs, Timothey 519
Rilker, William 644
Rillies, 232
Roads, Jacob 10
Roan, John 45
Robenson, Allexander 20
Robenson, John 20
Roberts, Morrice 298
Roberts, Morris 174, 504

Robins, William 118
Robinson, 518, 690, 755
Robinson, Alexander 1, 279
Robinson, David 616
Robinson, Job 640
Robinson, John 515
Robinson (Robison), Thomas 51, 53, 115, 198, 273, 304, 636, 654, 718
Rock, Wm 709
Rotton, John 416
Rowland, Thomas 141, 353, 354, 355
Rucker, Gideon 346
Rudasail, 158, 753
Rudasail, John 11
Rudasail, Mical 190
Rugsel, 99
Russel, George 580, 581, 582
Russell, Mathew 197
Rutherford, Griffith 207
Rutledg, Jas 623
Rutledge, 461, 710
Rutledge, Charles 723
Rutledge, George 44, 173, 202
Rutledge, James 212, 569, 655, 722, 723
Rutledge, John 44
Sailor, Soloman 644
Sailors, Conrad 676
Salaris, Zakariah 245
Salurs, Zakariah 466A
Saruc, John 49
Saterfield, 501
Satterfield, James 496, 497
Saunders, Richard 189, 197, 677, 744
Sayers, Charles 400, 402
Saylors, George 362
Sceigles, 728
Scenter, James 23, 157
Scenter, Jas sr 259, 715
Scenter, Stephen 613, 715, 720, 720A
Scott, Abraham 51, 273, 636,

Index to Tryon & Lincoln Co Land Entries 1779-1780

654, 718
Scott, Baptist   593
Scott, Gaskins   649
Scott, James   4, 145, 207, 299
Scott, John   206, 619
Scott, Joseph   759
Scott, Moses   173, 320, 346
Selmon, Frances   246
Senter, Jas   720A
Serhoeal, John   25
Shannon, Hugh   243, 644
Shannon, James   592, 612
Shannon, Joseph   60, 243
Sharp,   412, 474
Shaw, Benjamin   704
Shekil, John   131
Shilton, Joel   546, 547
Shilton, Stephen   75, 578, 579
Shipman, Joseph   519
Shitton, Stephen   75
Shrimshire, John   136
Shutley, Jacob   615
Sides, Jacob   240
Sides, Michael   622
Simons, Thomas   210, 210A
Sims,   605
Sims, Burrel   115, 520
Sims, Foster   451
Singleton, Richard   124, 125, 126, 663
Skremsin, John D   669
Skriggs,   310A
Skrimshire, John   339, 661, 700
Spriggs,   35, 36, 95
Spriggs, Thomas   94, 97, 420
Stacy, James   102
Stafford, John   373
Starret, William   3, 23
Stenson, Willian   40
Step, James   384, 404, 419
Storey,   494
Stuart, John   491
Suitar, William   289
Sullins, John   123
Sutton, Oliver   72

Skruggs, Richard   443
Sladen, Joseph   172
Slants, Charles F   39
Slants, Jacob   39
Sloan, James   76, 236, 242, 297
Sloan, John   16, 58, 62, 63, 70, 130, 171, 510, 661, 690, 714, 748, 749
Sloan, John sr   322
Smart, John   634
Smith, Catharine   7, 641
Smith, George   266
Smith, Jas   151
Smith, Jeremiah   190, 245, 480, 482, 606, 685
Smith, John   221, 258
Smith, Saml   672
Smith, William   147, 530, 611, 612, 615
Smith, William jr   321
Smith, William sr   312, 197, 637
Sorrel, John   383, 385, 541
Sorrels, John   112
Spencer,   478
Spencer, Joseph   553
Spencer, Saml   109, 110, 110A, 194, 195, 196, 200, 201, 228, 229, 284
Spencer, Zachariah   610, 637
Spencer, Zacorah   136
Sprigg,   427
Sprigg, Thomas   428
Swafford,   302
Swaffort,   571
Swamp, Maple   270, 271
Swan,   448
Swil, John   272
Tagert, Jno   712
Tagert, Violet   279
Tarter, Nicholass   681
Tarter, Palser   680
Taylor, Benjamin   193, 720
Taylor, George   376
Taylor, James   63, 180

Index to Tryon & Lincoln Co Land Entries 1779-1780

Taylor, John   133
Tery, William   469
Tesitty,   98
Thomas, Merryman   637
Thomason, George   358
Thomason, John   357, 392
Thomason, William   359
Thompson, David   237, 238
Thomson, James   276
Thremsin, John D   669
Torrance, Hugh   277, 575
Townsend,   152, 518
Townsend, Benjamin   358
Trout, George   63, 74, 713, 734
Trout, George jr   87
Trout, John   734
Tuaquers,   327
Tubbs (Tubb),   224, 323
Tubbs, William   237
Tucker, John   240, 705
Turner,   501
Turner, John   286, 430, 499
Turner, Samuel   500
Twitty,   98, 262, 381, 456
Vanzant,   39
Vanzant, Ferrard sr   684
Varner (Varnor, Vernor), William   453, 459, 688, 724
Vawn,   427
Vawn, Joseph   526
Waddelton,   597
Waddle, William   432
Wair, Robert   571
Walker,   30, 488
Walker, Collonell   285
Walker, John   231, 341, 342, 658, 665, 722, 723, 761
Wallace,   276, 312, 331, 592
Wallace, James   60
Walton, Nicholas   515
Walver, Christopher   304
Wamock, Abraham   728
Warlock,   729
Warren, Lott   450

Warren, Thomas   371, 449
Wasons,   330
Waterson, John   530
Watkins, John   761
Wear, John   67
Wear, Robert   69, 339
Weather (Weathers), John   38, 319
Webb, James   361, 430, 447
Webb, Jas jr   447
Webb, Jeremiah   520
Webb, John   440
Webb, Leonard   726, 727
Webb, Robert   520
Webb, William   372, 447
Wedlocks,   182
Welch, Thomas   57, 204
Well, Jeremiah   123
Wells, John   735
Wells, John sr   739
West,   461
West, Isaac   461
West, John   676
Wheat, widow   484
Whisinhunt, George   15
White,   310
White, James   149, 180, 222, 568
White, Orson   605
White, Samuel   444, 543
White, Soloman   479
White, Thomas   568
Whitenberg,   324
Whitesides,   120
Whitesides, James   127, 128, 129
Whitesides, Robert   663
Whitesides, Thomas   98, 559, 560
Whitesides, William   127, 128, 256
Whittenburg,   6
Wiatt, Daniel   715, 721
Wiatt, Daniel sr   437
Wiatt, James   437, 438
Wiatt, Thomas   235

Index to Tryon & Lincoln Co Land Entries 1779-1780

Wiatt, Vincent   22
Wilcocks,   353
Wilcocks, Isaac   407
Wilkins, William   346
Williams,   463
Williams, Benjamin   517
Williams, Giles   118
Williams, Jonis   348
Williams, Joseph   479
Williams, Meal 66
Williams, Moses   651, 670, 723
Willis, Stephen   541
Willis, William   211
Willis, William jr   221
Wills,   212
Wills, Alexander   555
Wills, Jno   722
Wilson, James   270
Wilson, John   508
Wilson, Jonathan   171
Wilson, Ralph   192
Winters,   347
Winters, George   107, 112, 116, 261
Wire, John   45, 83, 515, 699
Wire, Robert   45, 87, 154, 155, 156, 230, 239, 566, 605, 606, 616, 617, 712, 713, 734
Wire, Roler   230
Witherow, Jas   635
Branch, Bridges   614
Branch, Cabbin   679
Branch, Calf pen   159, 537
Branch, Camp   83, 113, 147, 154
Branch, Caney   32, 202, 648
Branch, Cants   130
Branch, Cherokee   126, 470
Branch, Chestnut Log   588
Branch, Cleghorns   532
Branch, Duncans   604
Branch, Falls   5, 30, 179
Branch, Fitzimon   662
Branch, Flat   263

Withrow, Jno   336
Wittenberg, Joseph   11
Wizenhant, George   566
Wood, John   121
Woodward, Warrich   74
Woodward, Warrick   63
Woodward, Warrick   681
Woolf, George 518
Wray, Wm   177
Wright, Moses   343, 344, 351
Wuker, Ike   92
Wyat, James   452
Wyatt, Daniel   724, 738
Wyatt, Daniel jr   259
Wyatt, Edmund   451, 724, 738
Wyatt, James   233, 235, 721, 724
Yancey, William   570
Young,   103
Young, John   144

Geographical locations
Big Meadows   47
Branch, Anches   14, 85
Branch, Andrews   39
Branch, Balls   355
Branch, Beaverdam   240, 733
Branch, Big   222, 313
Branch, Big Long   610
Branch, Big Meadow   317
Branch, Boreings   606
Branch, Bridge   624
Branch, Flat Rock   575
Branch, Frelands   67
Branch, Glady Meadow   513
Branch, Goffs   580, 633
Branch, Grassey   24
Branch, Green   445
Branch, Gressey   340
Branch, Grodfreys   488
Branch, Groves   329
Branch, Hicory   571
Branch, Hog Pen   574
Branch, Johnsons   493
Branch, Jumping   189, 324, 348, 357, 625, 677, 760

Index to Tryon & Lincoln Co Land Entries 1779-1780

Branch, Keeners 754
Branch, Kyrkonels 257
Branch, Lick 246, 709, 726, 763
Branch, Little 457
Branch, Locust Ridge 70, 326, 539
Branch, Logans 248
Branch, Long 87, 153, 172, 224, 241, 330, 393, 410, 451, 465, 529, 554, 566, 571, 620, 639, 671, 713, 721, 733, 734, 738, 756, 757
Branch, Magness 752
Branch, Marphego 67
Branch, McCashlands 658
Branch, McGaire 111
Branch, McInteres 175
Branch, McMurreys 471
Branch, Meadow 613
Branch, Metcalfs 494
Branch, Milbines 675
Branch, Mine 140
Branch, Moses 720A
Branch, Murpheys 699
Branch, Persimmon 68, 642, 749
Branch, Pipes 237
Branch, Pitsimon 439
Branch, Plant 227, 585
Branch, Pools 508
Branch, Popular 1, 624
Branch, Popular Spring 734
Branch, Pots 56
Branch, Reedy 112, 423
Branch, Ried 234
Branch, Rock Spring 235
Branch, Rockey 449
Branch, Shoal 391, 462
Branch, Sink hole 379
Branch, Skilwicker 228
Branch, Smith Shop 332
Branch, Tanyard 727
Branch, Thompson's Cabbin 717
Branch, Towsends 506

Branch, Turners 514
Branch, Uleys 134, 568
Branch, Vernors 744
Branch, Walkers (Walker) 11, 687
Branch, Welches 57
Branch, Williams 463
Branch, Wolf Pit 548
Branch, Wolf Trap 190, 714
Branch, Wolfs 272
Branch, Wyatts 715
Branch, Yanceys 497, 517
Cane Break 119
Charleston, SC 285, 482, 563
Cove, Little 110, 110A
Creek, Alstons 167, 194, 416
Creek, ashil 166
Creek, Ashworths 364, 365, 366, 367, 371, 430, 499
Creek, Bear 526
Creek, Beatys 254, 266
Creek, Beaver 500
Creek, Beaverdam 17-19, 82, 89, 129, 137, 177, 496, 501, 502, 546, 547, 584, 704, 707
Creek, Besons 84, 169, 172, 176, 671, 672, 673, 674, 731, 732, 758
Creek, Big Hicory 62, 81, 86, 322, 323, 356, 510, 530
Creek, Bills 567, 577, 578, 579, 595
Creek, Boreings 245, 551, 552
Creek, Bostons 720
Creek, Brier 213, 280, 281
Creek, Brights 354, 384, 421
Creek, Brushey 302
Creek, Buck 125
Creek, Buffalo 15, 16, 33, 34, 45, 46, 56, 58, 61, 63, 67-69, 71, 74, 76, 79, 83, 85, 87, 147, 148, 150, 153, 154, 156, 159, 175, 176, 182, 191, 195, 196, 218,

85

Index to Tryon & Lincoln Co Land Entries 1779-1780

232, 236, 241, 272, 274, 275, 284, 289, 297, 303, 307, 325-327, 330, 338, 432, 439, 463, 464-466, 515, 529, 537, 539, 540, 566, 571, 598, 609, 616, 620, 639, 642, 660-662, 699, 700, 701, 705, 706, 709, 711-714, 729, 730, 734, 748, 751, 756
Creek, Bullions 417, 538
Creek, Burshey 666
Creek, Byers 146
Creek, Cain 135, 145
Creek, Camp 305, 468, 602
Creek, Cane 635
Creek, Catheys 106, 113, 116, 346, 355, 388, 391, 467, 533, 565, 586
Creek, Cedar 107, 291, 348, 557, 594
Creek, Chalk hill 96
Creek, Cleghorne 349, 387, 523, 593
Creek, Coburns 668, 726, 727
Creek, Cove 93, 93A, 96, 119, 130, 138, 227, 375, 476, 477, 527, 534, 535, 557, 558, 577-579, 594, 595, 633, 634
Creek, Crowders 1, 5, 13, 20,
Creek. Grays 103
Creek, Greens 562
Creek, Grogg (Groog) 286, 368, 434
Creek, Hamptons Mill 351, 396
Creek, Harris 556
Creek, Hendersons 572
Creek, Hensons 186
Creek, Henteys 623
Creek, Hicory 466A
Creek, Hinsons 294
Creek, Hintons 288, 300, 559, 560
Creek, Horse 108, 350, 480
Creek, Howards 315, 518

26, 29, 40, 41, 47, 140, 151, 179, 183, 223, 244, 279, 317, 329, 486, 575, 614, 653, 683, 685, 687, 690, 743, 744, 755
Creek, Cummins 418
Creek, Cuninghams 198
Creek, Danebar 126
Creek, Darnalds 585
Creek, Delseys 369
Creek, Dillingers 746, 747
Creek, Doctors 622, 676
Creek, Doolys 282
Creek, Duharts 64, 243, 246, 265, 276, 312, 321, 331, 592, 612, 645, 686, 697, 698
Creek, Duncans (Dunkens) 251, 255, 256, 268
Creek, Dunharts 60
Creek, Durnalds 227
Creek, Dutchmans 23, 32, 44, 173, 202, 212, 240, 461, 569, 622, 644, 651, 652, 655, 678, 679, 710, 722, 723
Creek, Earricks 262
Creek, Floyds 184, 249, 359, 484, 601
Creek, Glaghorn 192
Creek, Goforth 279
Creek, Grants 477
Creek, Hoyles 8, 611, 615, 589, 691, 750, 762
Creek, Hughes 485
Creek, Indian 457, 458, 544, 545, 628, 629, 664, 703
Creek, James 220
Creek, Kain 102, 261, 263, 336, 341, 342
Creek, Killians 203, 745
Creek, Kings 31, 205. 314, 563, 717, 725, 735, 739, 742, 743
Creek, Kittle 736
Creek, Kyrkindals 267
Creek, Kittles 576
Creek, Leapers 669, 670

86

Index to Tryon & Lincoln Co Land Entries 1779-1780

Creek, Little   275, 279, 297, 424
Creek, Little Cain   97
Creek, Little Catawba   2, 12, 21, 42, 49, 54, 59, 65, 248, 277, 278, 313, 332, 431, 638, 640, 694, 695, 697, 719, 740, 741
Creek, Little Hicory   77, 174, 292, 298, 495, 504
Creek, Little Kane   428
Creek, Little Long   38, 233, 235, 437, 438, 444, 451-453, 459, 460, 543, 588
Creek, Little Shoal   78, 462
Creek, Long   6, 7, 10, 11, 22, 26-28, 37, 38, 57, 59, 63, 139, 149, 158, 177, 180, 189, 190, 197, 199, 204, 222, 226, 234, 318, 324, 568, 624, 641, 675, 677, 680-682, 692, 693, 708, 721, 738
Creek, Magness   87, 297, 339, 646, 647, 700
Creek, Maple   185, 345, 374, 378, 564
Creek, Marlins   210, 210A
Creek, Micals   316
Creek, Mill   54, 55, 100, 244, 309, 644, 719
Creek, Morris   476
Creek, Mountain   105, 111, 112, 347, 351, 352, 379, 382, 383, 385, 445, 475, 490, 541, 549. 562, 564, 599
Creek, Naked   328
Creek, Nawns   310A
Creek, Nob   309, 343, 344, 373, 403, 454
Creek, Potts   61, 239, 303, 716, 730
Creek, Puzzel   536
Creek, Richland   487
Creek, Ritchesons   144
Creek, Robinson (Robisiness)   214, 337, 391
Creek, Second   527
Creek, Seigles   728
Creek, Serrats   513, 514
Creek, Shekils   131, 132
Creek, Sheppards (Sheppords)   91, 335, 550, 630, 631, 632
Creek, Shoal (Shoals)   160, 524, 528, 573
Creek, Silver   73
Creek, Sizemores   357, 392
Creek, Skywicker (Skiewicker)   395, 425
Creek, Solomans   515
Creek, South   124, 250, 608, 663
Creek, upper Buffalo   252
Creek, Uptons Mill   301
Creek, Varons   426
Creek, Vawns   94, 427
Creek, Wades Mill 308
Creek, Walnut   206, 207, 215, 253, 299, 389, 597
Creek, Wards   304, 436
Creek, Webbs   521
Creek, Wheats   143, 353, 376, 394, 408
Creek, White Oak   121, 164, 165, 168, 187, 229, 301, 310, 398, 400-402, 407, 409, 410-415, 418-420, 469, 472, 474, 479, 542
Creek, Wilkeys   88, 89, 90
Creek, Williams (Wiliams)   155, 171, 553
Creek, Youngs   107
Court house, Tryon Co.   231, 439
Dears lick   183
Flat Rocks   238
Ford, Armstrong's   48
Ford, Beaty's   306
Ford, Blackwell's   188
Ford, Cove   567
Ford, Dides   493
Ford, Furasegah   621

Index to Tryon & Lincoln Co Land Entries 1779-1780

Ford, Hutson's   406
Ford, Island   481
Ford, Spencer's   38, 624, 675, 682
Ford, Turasegah   621
Fork, Chism   300
Fork, Corn field   546, 547
Fork, Glady   301
Fork, Jekins   400
Fork, Jenkins   410
Fork, Luck   232, 327
Fork, Muddy   17, 58, 63, 70, 74, 148, 153, 272, 325, 338, 432, 439, 465, 539, 540, 639, 660, 712, 748, 751, 752, 756
Fork, South   3, 43, 51, 53, 64, 133, 136, 157, 163, 178, 181, 193, 220, 226, 259, 273, 316, 319, 457, 458, 461, 544, 545, 576, 607, 611, 613, 637, 667, 684, 704, 706, 707, 715, 736, 737, 762, 763
Fork, Suck   605
Gap, Lively's   255
Island, Maple   667
Landing, Camp's   509   351, 352, 358, 359, 362, 368, 369, 373-377, 379-381, 383, 385, 387, 393, 403, 435, 440, 443, 445, 446, 454-456, 480, 481, 482, 484, 488, 490, 493, 499, 500, 503, 506-509, 511, 514, 515, 519, 522, 523, 531, 541, 548, 552, 570, 580-582, 590, 591, 593, 596, 600, 601, 603, 619, 635, 666, 714
River, Catawba   83, 198, 306, 320, 333, 471, 555, 569, 583, 621-623, 636, 637, 644, 649, 654, 696, 718, 726-728
River, First Broad   25, 78, 80, 88, 124-129, 171, 210, 210A, 211, 221, 230, 231,

Lick, Great   612
Meadows, Beaverdam   310
Meadows, Round   88
Mill, Capshaw's   310
Mill, Richardson's   433
Mill, Warlock's   729
Mountain, Bald   195
Mountain, Bills   567, 595
Mountain, Catawba   1
Mountain, Coals   250
Mountain, Hicory Nut   608
Mountain, Hoyl's   637
Mountain, Kings   563
Mountain, Laboon's   675
Mountain, Lasenbags   256
Mountain, Tryon   168, 395
Mountain, Young's   579
Muster ground, the   105
Path, More's   639
Punkin Roost   251
Ridge, Locust   17
River, Broad   50, 52, 98-100, 103, 111, 117, 118, 122, 141, 152, 155, 160, 182, 184, 188, 192, 195, 196, 216, 219, 232, 252, 263, 269, 284, 287, 293, 296, 308, 328, 343, 344, 348, 237, 238, 242, 245, 250, 251, 254-258, 266, 268, 280, 281, 288, 292, 294, 298, 300, 302, 309, 322, 334, 340, 436, 441, 442, 501, 502, 504, 510, 517, 553, 556, 559, 560, 570, 584, 605, 606, 608, 617, 626, 643, 663
River, Green   72, 73, 95A, 104, 109-110A, 120, 142, 161, 162, 167, 194, 200, 201, 206, 207, 215, 253, 282, 283, 295, 299, 353, 354, 384, 386, 397, 398, 399, 404-407, 416, 417, 419, 421, 422, 473, 478, 487, 489, 491, 494, 498, 538,

Index to Tryon & Lincoln Co Land Entries 1779-1780

   542, 561, 597, 618
River, Little Broad   75, 123,
   224, 225, 247, 264, 423,
   433, 496, 497, 524, 528,
   546, 547
River, N Pacolet   92, 94, 95,
   97, 108, 165, 186, 217, 228,
   350, 424-426, 428, 429, 485,
   492, 510, 526
River, Pacolet   35
River, Second Broad   114,
   145, 208, 209, 305, 341,
   342, 346, 355, 357, 360,
   361, 364-367, 370, 371,
   392, 430, 434, 443, 447,
   448, 449, 470, 520, 521,
   536, 565, 572, 573, 574,
   587, 604, 656, 657, 658, 665
Road, Cove   490
Road, Gilbert's   122, 482
Road, Green's   642
Road, Ridge   59
Road, Walker's   590
Rock house, the   399
Rock House Bottom   252
Run, Crooked   25
Run, Roaring   607
Run, Sandy   216, 285, 311,
   334, 368, 455, 483, 511,
   512, 519, 589-591, 659
Run, Shoal   660
School house, the   393
Shoal, Buck   188
Shoal, Hawkins   507
Shoals, Island fork   287
South Carlonia, line   503, 513,
   526, 709
Spring, Camp   160
Spring, Holy   257
Spring, Rock   574, 688
Table, Great   395

www.ingramcontent.com/pod-product-compliance
Lightning Source LLC
Chambersburg PA
CBHW031427290426
44110CB00011B/551